Safety in the use
of mineral and synthetic fibres

OCCUPATIONAL SAFETY
AND HEALTH SERIES
No. 64

SAFETY IN THE USE
OF MINERAL AND SYNTHETIC FIBRES

Working document and Report of the Meeting of
Experts on Safety in the Use of Mineral and
Synthetic Fibres, Geneva, 17-25 April 1989

An ILO contribution to the
International Programme on Chemical Safety
(a collaborative programme of the United Nations
Environment Programme,
the International Labour Organisation,
and the World Health Organization)

INTERNATIONAL LABOUR OFFICE   GENEVA

ISBN 92-2-106443-3
ISSN 0078-3129

First published 1990

Published in French under the title:
Sécurité dans l'utilisation des fibres minérales et synthétiques (ISBN 92-2-206443-7), Geneva, 1990

Aso published in Spanish under the title:
Seguridad en la utilización de fibras minerales y sintéticas (ISBN 92-2-306443-7), Geneva, 1990

Printed by the International Labour Office, Geneva, Switzerland

CONTENTS

1. INTRODUCTION

At its 72nd Session (June 1986), when adopting the Asbestos Convention, 1986 (No. 162), and Recommendation (No. 172), the International Labour Conference expressed its concern about the health effects of occupational exposure to other fibrous materials. Consequently, it adopted a resolution concerning the development of preventive and protective measures related to health risks associated with occupational exposure to fibres, whether natural or artificial (see Annex 1). It requested the Director-General, inter alia, to set up a tripartite group of experts to study the question of occupational health risks due to exposure to fibres, whether natural or artificial, other than asbestos, and to advise the Office and the Governing Body on action to be taken to protect workers against occupational exposure to mineral and synthetic fibres. The Governing Body at its 239th Session (February–March 1988) approved the holding of the meeting from 17 to 25 April 1989.

The resolution also requested the Director-General to expedite the health risk assessment of inorganic fibres, whether natural or artificial, other than asbestos, currently under way by the International Programme on Chemical Safety (IPCS), executed jointly by the United Nations Environmental Programme, the International Labour Office and the World Health Organization. This assessment has been completed and published by the WHO as Environmental Health Criteria 77, Man-made mineral fibres (1988).

There is a wide range of products which could be classified as synthetic fibres. For the purpose of this document, it was agreed to follow the definition of man-made fibres given in the ILO's Encyclopaedia of occupational health and safety (third edition, 1983). Man-made fibres are divided into synthetic fibres, in which the fibre-forming material is derived from monomeric chemicals (organic synthetic fibres) or from minerals (man-made mineral fibres), and artificial fibres, in which the fibre-forming material is of natural vegetable or animal origin such as viscose rayon fibres, cellulose ester fibres or protein fibres. In conformity with the terms of reference of the Meeting of Experts, artificial fibres of vegetable or animal origin are not discussed in this document.

The present document discusses safety and health in the use of mineral and synthetic fibres at work, taking due account of the relevant international instruments, in particular the Occupational Safety and Health Convention, 1981 (No. 155), and

Recommendation (No. 164), the Working Environment (Air Pollution, Noise and Vibration) Convention, 1977 (No. 148), and Recommendation (No. 156), and the Asbestos Convention, 1986 (No. 162), and Recommendation (No. 172), as well as the ILO code of practice, Safety in the use of asbestos, published in 1984.

The first three chapters deal with man-made mineral fibres, natural mineral fibrous materials and organic synthetic fibres, and with their health effects. The following chapters discuss preventive and control measures, and law and practice in selected countries. The main resources for the risk assessment were the WHO/IARC Monographs on the Evaluation of the Carcinogenic Risk of Chemicals to Humans, Vol. 42: Silica and some silicates (1987), and Vol. 43: Man-made mineral fibres and radon (1988), and for the risk evaluation the WHO Environmental Health Criteria 53, Asbestos and other natural mineral fibres (1986) and 77 Man-made mineral fibres (1988).

The document aims at providing basic information to all concerned when implementing safety in the use of mineral and synthetic fibres other than asbestos. It covers a wide range of materials:

(i)   man-made mineral fibres - insulation wools (rockwool, slagwool and glasswool); refractory (including ceramic) fibres; continuous filament glass fibres; and special purpose fibres;

(ii)   natural mineral fibres other than asbestos - erionite, attapulgite, and wollastonite;

(iii)   synthetic organic fibres - aramid fibres; carbon and graphite fibres, and polyolefin fibres.

These materials have two important features in common:

(i)   they are all fibrous materials, with most containing, to a greater or lesser extent, respirable fibres; and

(ii)   their production and use (with the exception of erionite) is increasing throughout the world.

The definition of respirable fibres used in this text is that published in the ILO code of practice, Safety in the use of asbestos: "a particle with a diameter of less than 3 μm and of which the length is at least three times the diameter". But the Meeting of Experts expressed concern that this definition of respirable fibre did not adequately describe those fibres which were currently thought to pose the greatest hazard. Since research has suggested that fibres of less than 1.5 μm diameter, more than 5 μm length, and length to diameter ratios of more than 5:1 were more likely to be hazardous, the Meeting believed that a redefinition of respirable fibre was needed. However, such a redefinition was not within the scope of the Meeting of Experts.

The production and use of these materials is rapidly expanding, and research into their health effects is continuing. Additionally, new materials and products, as well as manufacturing technologies, are being developed and invented. For these reasons, the information provided in this report, while reflecting current knowledge, must be regularly reviewed as new data become available. The Meeting of Experts strongly encouraged the continuation of research and the generation of more data.

2. MAN-MADE MINERAL FIBRES

2.1 General

Man-made mineral fibres (MMMF), most of which are referred to as man-made vitreous fibres, or synthetic mineral/vitreous fibres, have been manufactured and used for over 100 years. There are different types of MMMF such as insulation wool (including glasswool, mineral wool, rockwool and slagwool), refractory (including ceramic) fibres, continuous filament and special purpose fibres (table 1).[1]

Table 1. Classification, methods of manufacture, and nominal diameters of MMMF

	Man-made mineral fibres			
	Continuous filament	Insulation wool	Refractory fibres	Special-purpose fibres
	(1) Glass	(1) Glasswool (2) Rockwool (3) Slagwool	(1) Ceramic (2) Others	(1) Glass microfibres
Nominal fibre diameters[A]	6-15 μm	2-9 μm	1.2-3 μm	0.1-3 μm
	Drawn	Centrifuged Centrifuged/blown	Blown Drawn/blown	Flame attenuated
	Method of manufacture			

[A] Approximate range of mean diameters.

The different types of MMMF have provided great benefits to society through their uses in home, office and factory thermal insulation, energy conservation, acoustic insulation, fire-proofing and fire protection, domestic appliance insulation, aerospace insulation, and as reinforcing materials in plastics, plasters, cement and textiles.

On the other hand, the exposure of workers to excessive concentrations of airborne dust of MMMF has raised serious concern about possible harmful effects on their health, concern supported by the results of animal experiments and some epidemiological evidence. Skin, eye and upper-respiratory-tract irritation in people exposed to high concentrations of MMMF has been known for decades. Only more recently has it been realised that airborne MMMF can be of such small dimension as to become respirable and be deposited in the lung tissue. Therefore, it has been questioned whether MMMF could not have effects similar to those caused by excessive exposure to the dust of asbestos, i.e. causing lung fibrosis, bronchial cancer or mesothelioma of the pleura and peritoneum.

Some of the MMMF contain fibres with diameters in the respirable range which can, under certain circumstances, be released into the air during manufacture and use. Because of this, extensive research has been carried out during the past 20 years into the short- and long-term health effects of MMMF, in particular cancer of the respiratory system. While the research has not yet answered all the questions about possible effects, it has provided sufficiently reliable data on which to develop practical policies on control measures in the manufacture and use of some MMMF, in particular insulation wools and continuous filaments. However, there is a lack of information on refractory and special purpose fibres.

2.2 Characteristics

Most of the MMMF are amorphous silicates, in contrast to naturally occurring fibrous minerals which are crystalline in structure. Because of this they do not split longitudinally into fibres of smaller diameter, but may break transversely into shorter segments. The world production of MMMF is not accurately known but estimates indicate that current production is in the order of 7 million tonnes per annum. The chemical composition of the different fibre types varies, as do the length and diameters of the fibres. These differences have an important bearing on the potential for the fibres to be inhaled into and retained in the lungs.

Most insulation wools contain binders and dust-suppressing agents. The binders are primarily phenol-formaldehyde resins; however, some are urea-formaldehyde resins. These are sprayed on the fibre mass in the early stages of production. Binders and dust-suppressing agents are not used in finished refractory fibre products. Products without binders and dust-suppressing agents are likely to generate more airborne respirable fibres during manufacture and use than products containing binders and dust-suppressing agents.

MMMF are manufactured to specific nominal diameters which vary according to fibre type and use. Insulation wools are usually made to nominal diameters ranging from 2 to 9 μm; refractory fibres from 1.2 to 3 μm; special purpose fibres from

0.1 to 3 μm; and continuous filament fibres from 6 to 15 μm. In any bulk sample of insulation wool there will be fibres several times greater than and less than the nominal diameter.

2.3 Manufacturing methods

2.3.1 General

There have been changes in the principles of manufacturing processes over time. Manufacturing methods have also been refined and have become more efficient, enabling significant improvements to be made in the final product.

The manufacturing processes include drawing, blowing and spinning (centrifuging) alone or in combination, but all begin with melts of raw materials which vary according to the requirements of composition and characteristics for the final product. The techniques used to melt are cupola, gas or electric furnace or electrode bath furnace. Most melts to be fiberised require temperatures in the range of 1200°C and 1600°C, although refractory fibres require higher temperatures.

Only drawing has the potential for close control of the diameter of the fibres. This method produces continuous filaments within a narrow diameter range. Drawing begins by forcing the melt through a plate with a number of very small holes. The strands (filaments) are stretched while still in a soft state, then combed together and wound on a bobbin for further processing. The diameter of the fibre is controlled by the melt viscosity, the size of the plate holes and the speed of the bobbin winding. All of these are relatively easily manipulated and allow fine control of the filament diameter, with a tolerance of 10 per cent.

Spinning (sometimes referred to as centrifuging) involves pouring a stream of molten material on to rapidly spinning wheels. A number of configurations have been developed to cope with the requirements of the final product. The molten material is flung between and off the wheels by centrifugal action. As a globule of molten material leaves the wheel it forms a small head (sometimes referred to as "shot") and a long tail or fibre. This method produces fibres of varying diameter and length, depending on melt characteristics, spin velocity, pour speed of the melt and the general surface conditions of the wheel.

Fiberisation with a single disc is also used with or without the aid of air or steam blowing axially near the edge and thus elongating the fibres created while the melt is flung from the disc by the centrifugal force.

Blowing is a process in which the range of fibre diameters could be difficult to control. In its crude form, this technique of fiberisation lets a stream of melt be poured, passing in front of a jet of air or steam which blows into a collecting chamber. The jet splits the melt stream into fibres and more or less globular particles, or "shots". Blowing is less efficient than spinning, giving a larger proportion of shots.

Rotation and blowing are also combined in processes where the melt is fed into the interior of a hollow, rotating cup, with a large number of holes in the peripheral wall. Usually, streams of combustion gases are used to fiberise the melt as it is forced out through the holes by the centrifugal force.

Today, more refined blowing processes have been developed. In one important process, the glass to be fiberised is fed as thin glass rods to flames. This fiberises the glass in a controllable way without producing shots (flame attenuation process). This is the most important process for the production of superfine and special purpose fibres.

Dust-suppressing agents are added to almost all insulation wools at the collection stage, immediately after the fiberisation process and before the fibres have formed a blanket. Materials that are used as dust suppressants include both mineral and/or vegetable oils and waxes. Where MMMF products are expected to resist high temperatures (e.g. refractory ceramic fibre), such dust-suppression agents are burnt out prior to packaging.

2.3.2 Glassfibres

There are three main types of glassfibres: continuous filament, insulation wool and special purpose fibres. They are composed primarily of the oxides of silicon, calcium, sodium, potassium aluminium and boron. Silica sand, limestone, dolomite, boron oxide, fluorspar and glass fragments (cullets) provide the main raw materials. During production, the composition can be changed to promote specific properties.[2]

2.3.3 Rockwool and slagwool

Rockwool and slagwool are insulation wools manufactured from melted magmatic rock and slagwool produced from melted slag from metallurgical processes such as iron, steel or copper production. Rockwool and slagwool consist mainly of oxides of silicon, aluminium, calcium and magnesium but they also contain some iron oxide. The chemical resistance and the solubility in water of rockwool and slagwool varies widely.[2]

2.3.4 Refractory fibres

Refractory fibres, including ceramic fibres, comprise a large group of amorphous or partially crystalline synthetic mineral fibres that are highly refractory. They are produced from kaolin clay or the oxides of alumina, silicon or other metals, or less commonly from non-oxide materials such as silicon carbide, silicon nitride or boron nitride. Increased temperature resistance is achieved by the addition of greater quantities of alumina. While they have an amorphous structure when produced, some conversion to other crystalline forms of silica, such as cristobalite and mullite, can occur over time at temperatures around 1000°C. [3]

2.4 Occupational exposure

2.4.1 General

MMMF have a wide range of uses, which means that many people are exposed to them at work. Continuous filament glassfibres are used in the reinforcement of cement, plaster and plastic materials, in paper and rubber products, in industrial textiles and in electrical insulation. Insulation wools are used in thermal and acoustic insulation (domestic and industrial), in acoustic ceiling tiles and panels, in ventilation and air-conditioning ducts and in fire proofing and fire protection. Refractory fibres are used in high temperature insulation; in fire proofing and fire protection; and in interpenetrations in buildings. Both insulation wools and refractory fibres are used as components in friction materials. Special purpose glassfibres are used in high-performance insulation, particularly in the aerospace industry, in high-performance acoustic protection, and in high-efficiency filtration.

The type of MMMF used in thermal insulation depends on the temperature resistance of the fibres. Most glasswools are limited to a maximum service temperature of 450°C, though recently developed glasswool may service up to 800°C. Rockwool and slagwool are limited to a maximum service temperature of 820°C. Ceramic fibre can service temperatures above 820°C. Aluminium silicate ceramic fibres are limited to a maximum service temperature of 1300°C, but high alumina fibres are available for use up to 1600°C. Product performance (thermal conductivity) is primarily a function of fibre diameter. As fibre diameter increases, product performance is reduced.

2.4.2 Continuous filament glassfibres

Because these products are manufactured to diameters ranging from 6 to 20 μm, there are no respirable glass filament fibres associated with them. Total dust concentrations can be high in industries using this product and the dusts are very irritating because they contain non-respirable fibres and non-fibrous particles. Besides engineering control measures, the use of respiratory protective equipment and safety goggles is frequently necessary when cutting, grinding, or sanding products containing continuous filament glass fibre such as fibre-reinforced plastics, e.g. boats, pools, baths, sinks, plumbing and roof sheets or tiles, and fibre-reinforced plaster products.

Associated chemical exposures and the need for their control are also important. In manufacture, formaldehyde resin systems are used. In the use of continuous filament glassfibres for reinforced plastic products, associated chemicals include polyester resins, cobalt naphthenates, and methyl ethyl ketone peroxides.

2.4.3 Insulation wools

In the manufacture of insulation wools (glasswool, rockwool and slagwool) total dust concentrations are rarely elevated above the generally accepted exposure limits. Respirable fibre concentrations are mostly below 1 f/ml. Formaldehyde resins are used as binders, and formaldehyde concentrations may be elevated.

In the installation of insulation, measured airborne respirable fibre levels are likewise usually low; most values are less than 1 f/ml, but occasional levels in confined spaces have been found in the range of 1 to 2 f/ml.

Handling of insulation wool products occupies only part of the working day, hence the time-weighted average concentrations of fibres during a full working day are usually lower than those observed during the actual installation. Total dust levels usually are low. However due to other activities on the building sites, total dust levels can be higher than in manufacturing plants. The IPCS[1] has evaluated that in general, airborne fibre concentrations during the installation of products containing MMMF are comparable to, or less than, levels found in production, i.e. less than 1 f/ml. Exceptions occur during blowing or spraying operations conducted in confined spaces, such as during the insulation of aircraft or attics, when mean levels of fibrous glass and mineral wool have ranged up to 1.8 f/ml and 4.2 f/ml, respectively. Mean concentrations during installation of loose fill in confined spaces have ranged up to 8.2 f/ml.

Demolition of structures containing friable insulation wools may cause high levels of airborne dust or fibres.

Thermal breakdown of the dust suppressant agents and binder results in increased dustiness. This can also be the case with old insulation especially if it has collected other dust during the years. The removal of old or heated insulation can therefore create more respirable dust than the installation.

Elevated concentrations of airborne fibres can be found in spraying and in some cleaning operations. Normally these are accompanied by very high concentrations of total dust, caused in particular by the cement used in the spraying process.

2.4.4 Refractory fibres

Because the product does not contain a binder, respirable fibre levels tend to be higher in refractory fibre manufacture than in the manufacture of insulation wools. Concentrations exceeding 1 f/ml have been reported.[1] Total dust concentrations are usually less than 2 mg/m^3. Because binders are not used, formaldehyde is not a problem.

Unpublished measurements from industry and government agencies have shown that fire rating of firewalls, rated ceilings, interpenetrations, and fire doors with refractory fibre batts can result in airborne respirable fibre concentrations of less than 1 f/ml and total dust concentrations up to 5 mg/m^3. Installation of high temperature insulation such as furnace lining and pipe lagging can result in respirable fibre levels in excess of 1 f/ml, with total dust concentrations being usually less than 2 mg/m^3. Removal of high temperature insulation can result in very high respirable fibre levels, well in excess of 1.0 f/ml (unpublished industry data). The total dust concentration can also be very high, and cristobalite and mullite may be present.

2.4.5 Special purpose glassfibres

There is little available information on airborne respirable fibre levels during manufacture. Because this product is made to a nominal diameter of 1.0 μm or less and binders are not used, strict controls are necessary to keep levels below 1.0 f/ml. Total dust concentrations are low. Average airborne concentration in speciality fine fibre plants range from 1 to 2 f/ml, and concentrations are highest (1 to 50 f/ml) in microfibre production facilities.[1]

Special purpose insulation, as used in the aerospace industry, has resulted in low total dust concentrations but high airborne respirable fibre levels.

2.5 Non-occupational exposure

Insulation wools are widely used for home insulation and are often installed by the householder. Airborne respirable fibre levels are low when bonded products in batt form are used, usually of the order of 0.1 f/ml or less. Total dust levels, however, may be as high as 10mg/m^3 or more, especially when the insulation material is installed in old homes. Skin irritation can be minimised by wearing gloves, loose-fitting long-sleeved shirts and long trousers, and by tucking a cloth inside the collar. Eye protection, in the form of safety goggles, should be worn.

Continuous filament glassfibres are also used in many homes in the use of reinforced plastics in boat building and hobbies. Total dust levels can be high, particularly if power tools are used for cutting or sanding but respirable fibre levels are considered not to be a problem because of the coarse diameter (greater than 6 μm) of the continuous filament glassfibre. Associated chemical exposures may be high if the tasks are carried out in poorly ventilated areas. Skin irritation can be minimised if gloves, loose-fitting, long-sleeved shirts and long trousers are worn, and if a cloth is tucked inside the collar. Chemical exposures should be minimised by increased ventilation and the use of an approved respirator.

2.6 Health effects

2.6.1 General

The results of the extensive research into health effects have been presented at two international conferences organised by the World Health Organization in Copenhagen in 1982[4] and 1986.[5] The health effects associated with occupational and environmental exposure to MMMF have been evaluated by the International Programme on Chemical Safety (IPCS),[1] and an evaluation of the carcinogenicity of MMMF has been conducted by the International Agency for Research on Cancer (IARC).[6]

2.6.2 Irritant effects

Skin irritation can be caused by fibres with diameters greater than about 4.5-5.0 μm, such as most insulation wools and continuous filament glassfibres. The mechanical irritation of the fibres results in an irritant dermatitis which may be complicated by an urticarial and eczematous reaction. In general, the dermatitis is not severe and does not last long.[7,8]

In addition, allergic reactions to resins used in MMMF production occasionally occur.[1]

Eye irritation has also been reported[9] and is associated with both coarse fibres which come into contact with the eye, and with other non-fibrous dusts often present where MMMF are used.

2.6.3 Non-malignant respiratory disease including fibrosis

(i) Effects on humans

Available data on non-malignant respiratory disease in populations occupationally exposed to MMMF were summarised by the IPCS[1] as follows:

> Some cross-sectional epidemiological studies suggest that there may be MMMF-exposure-related effects on respiratory function; others do not. In a large, well-conducted study, there was an increase in the prevalence of low profusion small shadowing on the chest radiographs of cigarette smokers with increasing length of employment in MMMF manufacturing. However, no consistent pattern of MMMF-related non-malignant effects on the respiratory system has emerged, to date, from cross-sectional surveys.

> There has been little evidence of excess mortality from non-malignant respiratory disease (NMRD) in MMMF workers in analytical epidemiological studies that have been conducted to date, including the two largest investigations conducted in Europe and the United States. There were no statistically significant increases in NMRD mortality in any sector of the industry in comparison with local rates ... The mortality rates were not related either to time since first exposure or to duration or intensity of exposure.

No published reports of studies of people exposed to refractory fibres have been found.

(ii) Effects on experimental animals

The results of experimental studies on non-malignant disease in animals were also summarised by the IPCS as follows:[1]

> In the majority of the inhalation studies conducted to date, there has been little or no evidence of fibrosis of the lungs in a range of animal species exposed to concentrations of various types of MMMF. (Editor's note: rockwool, slagwool, glasswool, special purpose glassfibres.) In most studies, the tissue response was confined to accumulation of pulmonary macrophages, many of which contained the fibres. In all cases, the severity of

the tissue reaction in animals exposed to special purpose glassfibre and, in one study, glasswool, was much less than that for equal masses of chrysotile or crocidolite asbestos. Moreover, in contrast to asbestos, fibrosis did not progress following cessation of exposure. However, the number of asbestos fibres reaching the lung may have been greater than those for fibrous glass and glasswool.

There has been some evidence of fibrosis in various species, following intratracheal administration of special purpose glassfibres. However, in most cases, the tissue response has been confined to an inflammatory reaction.

Inhalation or intrapleural injection of aluminium oxide refractory fibre containing about 4 per cent silica caused minimal pulmonary reaction in rats. On the other hand, the incidence of interstitial fibrosis following the inhalation of fibrous ceramic aluminium silicate glass was similar to that for chrysotile exposed animals. (Editor's note: based on the results of one study.)

2.6.4 Malignant respiratory disease

(i) Effects on humans

The epidemiological data on cancer mortality and incidence in people exposed to MMMF were summarised by the IPCS as follows:[1]

(a) Insulation wools (glasswool, rockwool, slagwool)

An excess of mortality due to lung cancer has been observed in the large epidemiological studies on rockwool/slagwool production workers conducted in Europe and the United States, but not in studies on glasswool. The excess of lung cancer mortality and/or incidence in the rockwool/slagwool production industry was ... statistically significant in the United States study and not statistically significant in the European study. There was a relationship (not statistically significant) with time from first exposure in the European study, but not in the United States study. No relationships with duration of employment or estimated cumulative exposure to fibres were observed. In the European study, a statistically significant excess of lung cancer was found in workers in the "early technological phase", during which airborne fibre levels were estimated to have been higher than in later production phases. A statistically significant increase in lung cancer mortality in the European study, 20 years after first exposure, appeared to be associated with the use of slag, but there was a large overlap between the use of slag and the early technological phase. Neither the use of bitumen and pitch nor the presence of asbestos in some products accounted for the observed lung cancer excess. In the European study, there was no excess lung cancer mortality in rockwool/slagwool production workers employed in the "late technological phase", when concentrations of fibres were thought to be lower after the full introduction of dust-suppressing agents.

For glasswool production workers, there were no excesses of lung cancer mortality compared with local rates in either the large European or United States cohorts. In both investigations, mortality from respiratory cancer showed an increase with time from first exposure that was not statistically significant. However, it was not related to duration of employment or estimated cumulative fibre exposure in the United States study, or to different technological phases in the European study. The standard mortality rate (SMR) for respiratory cancer, in workers who had been exposed in the manufacture of small diameter (less than 3 um) glassfibres in the United States cohort, was elevated compared with that in those who had never been exposed in this production sector. The excess in these workers was related to time from first exposure, but neither the overall increase nor the time trends were statistically significant. A statistically significant large excess of lung cancer, observed in a smaller Canadian cohort of glasswool production workers, was not related to time since first exposure or duration of employment.

There has not been any evidence, in studies conducted to date, that pleural or peritoneal mesotheliomas are associated with occupational exposures to insulation wools.

(b) Continuous filament

There has not been an increase in the mortality or incidence of lung cancer or mesothelioma in continuous filament production workers in studies conducted to date.

(c) Refractory fibres

No epidemiological data are available on the mortality or incidence of lung cancer or mesothelioma in refractory fibre workers.

(ii) Effects on experimental animals

The results of experimental studies of malignant disease in animals were summarised by the IPCS.[1] Because of lack of relevant detail in the publication of the studies, it was difficult to make clear distinctions between fibre types, though most of the experimental data relate to special purpose fibres:

A statistically significant increase in lung tumours has not been found in animals exposed to glassfibres (including special purpose fibres) or rockwool in inhalation studies conducted to date. However, in several of the relevant studies, an increase in lung tumours that was not statistically significant was found in exposed animals. In all of the carcinogenicity bioassays conducted to date, similar mass concentrations of chrysotile asbestos have clearly induced lung tumours, whereas crocidolite asbestos has induced few or no tumours. However, available data are insufficient to draw conclusions concerning the relative potency of various fibre types, because the true exposure (number of respirable fibres) was not characterised in most of these studies.

An increased incidence of lung tumours has been reported following intratracheal administration of special purpose fibres to two species in the same laboratory, but these results have not been confirmed by other investigators.

Studies involving intrapleural or intraperitoneal administration of MMMF to animals have provided information on the importance of fibre size and in vivo durability in the induction of fibrosis and neoplasia. The probability of the development of mesotheliomas following intrapleural and intraperitoneal administration of these dusts was best correlated with the number of fibres with diameters of less than 0.25 µm and lengths greater than 8 µm; however, probabilities were also relatively high for fibres with diameters of less than 1.5 µm and lengths greater than 4 µm. A model in which the carcinogenic potency of fibres is considered to be a continuous function of length and diameter and also of stability has been proposed. Asbestos has been more potent than equal masses of glassfibre in inducing tumours following intrapleural administration. However, certain types of ceramic fibres were as potent as equal masses of crocidolite asbestos in inducing mesotheliomas after intraperitoneal injection. A similar tumour response was observed after intraperitoneal injection of a comparable number of actinolite asbestos fibres longer than 5 µm, basalt wool, and ceramic wool.

Inhalation or intrapleural injection of aluminium oxide refractory fibre containing about 4 per cent silica caused no pulmonary neoplasms in rats. On the other hand, the incidence of pulmonary neoplasms following the inhalation of fibrous ceramic aluminium silicate glass was similar to that for chrysotile-exposed animals; however, half of the induced tumours were not typical of those observed in animals exposed to asbestos. (Editor's note: based on the results of one study.)

2.6.5 <u>Other relevant factors</u>

Other factors relevant to the evaluation of potential health risks associated with exposure to MMMF were summarised by IARC[6] as follows. (Editor's note: in IARC monograph,[6] the term "glasswool" comprises both glasswool and special purpose fibres.)

Many samples of man-made mineral fibres with large fibre diameter have low respirability.

The solubility of man-made mineral fibres <u>in vitro</u> and their durability <u>in vivo</u> vary with chemical composition. While, in general, glasswool fibres appear to be relatively non-durable, one sample (editor's note: fibres of alkali free borosilicate glass) was shown to be very insoluble <u>in vitro</u>. Conversely, while in one study ceramic fibres were very durable, one sample proved to be as soluble as glasswool used for comparison in the same experiment <u>in vitro</u>. Insufficient samples of slagwool and rockwool have been tested to allow a prediction of their overall range of solubility in tissues. On the available evidence, no generalisation can be made regarding the durability of any single class of man-made mineral fibres.

Glasswool induced numerical and structural chromosomal alterations but not sister chromatid exchanges in mammalian cells <u>in vitro</u>. It caused morphological transformation in rodent cells <u>in vitro</u>; transformation was found to be dependent on fibre length and diameter. Glasswool did not induce mutation in bacteria.

Ceramic fibres caused a weak response in an assay for morphological transformation but did not induce DNA damage in mouse cells <u>in vitro</u>.

No adequate data on genetic and related effects of rockwool and slagwool were available.

2.6.6 <u>IARC evaluation</u>[6]

    (a) <u>Rockwool/slagwool</u>

There is <u>limited evidence</u> for the carcinogenicity of rockwool/slagwool in humans.

There is <u>limited evidence</u> for the carcinogenicity of rockwool in experimental animals.

There is <u>inadequate evidence</u> for the carcinogenicity of slagwool in experimental animals.

<u>Overall evaluation</u>: rockwool and slagwool are possibly carcinogenic to humans (Group 2B).

    (b) <u>Glasswool (including special purpose fibres)</u>

There is <u>inadequate evidence</u> for the carcinogenicity of glasswool in humans.

There is <u>sufficient evidence</u> for the carcinogenicity of glasswool in experimental animals.

<u>Overall evaluation</u>: Glasswool is <u>possibly carcinogenic</u> to humans (Group 2B).

    (c) <u>Continuous filament</u>

There is <u>inadequate evidence</u> for the carcinogenicity of continuous (glass) filament in humans.

There is <u>inadequate evidence</u> for the carcinogenicity of continuous (glass) filament in experimental animals.

<u>Overall evaluation</u>: Continuous (glass) filaments are <u>not classifiable</u> as to their carcinogenicity to humans (Group 3).

    (d) <u>Refractory (ceramic) fibres</u>

No data were available on the carcinogenicity of refractory (ceramic) fibres to humans.

There is <u>sufficient evidence</u> for the carcinogenicity of refractory (ceramic) fibres in experimental animals.

<u>Overall evaluation</u>: Refractory (ceramic) fibres are <u>possibly carcinogenic</u> to humans (Group 2B).

[Note: The IARC[6] provides the following definition of the categories of carcinogenicity:

Group 1 – The agent is carcinogenic to humans.

This category is used only when there is <u>sufficient evidence</u> of carcinogenicity in humans.

Group 2

This category includes agents for which, at one extreme, the degree of evidence of carcinogenicity in humans is almost sufficient, as well as agents for which, at the other extreme, there are no human data but for which there is experimental evidence of carcinogenicity. Agents are assigned to either 2A (probably carcinogenic) or 2B (possibly carcinogenic) on the basis of epidemiological, experimental and other relevant data.

Group 2A – The agent is probably carcinogenic to humans.

This category is used when there is <u>limited evidence</u> of carcinogenicity in humans and <u>sufficient evidence</u> of carcinogenicity in experimental animals. Exceptionally, an agent may be classified into this category solely on the basis of <u>limited evidence</u> of carcinogenicity in humans or of <u>sufficient evidence</u> of carcinogenicity in experimental animals strengthened by supporting evidence from other relevant data.

Group 2B – The agent is possibly carcinogenic to humans.

This category is generally used for agents for which there is <u>limited evidence</u> in humans in the absence of <u>sufficient evidence</u> in experimental animals. It may also be used when there is <u>inadequate evidence</u> of carcinogenicity in humans or when human data are non-existent but there is <u>sufficient evidence</u> of carcinogenicity in experimental animals. In some instances, an agent for which there is <u>inadequate evidence</u> or no data in humans but <u>limited evidence</u> of carcinogenicity in experimental animals together with supporting evidence from other relevant data may be placed in this group.

Group 3 – The agent is not classifiable as to its carcinogenicity to humans.

Agents are placed in this category when they do not fall into any other group.

<u>Group 4</u> - The agent is probably not carcinogenic to humans.

This category is used for agents for which there is <u>evidence suggesting lack of carcinogenicity</u> in humans together with <u>evidence suggesting lack of carcinogenicity</u> in experimental animals. In some circumstances, agents for which there is <u>inadequate evidence</u> of or no data on carcinogenicity in humans but <u>evidence suggesting lack of carcinogenicity</u> in experimental animals, consistently and strongly supported by a broad range of other relevant data, may be classified in this group.]

2.7 <u>Evaluation of human health risks</u>

The human health risks in the occupational and non-occupational environment were evaluated by the IPCS as follows:[1]

2.7.1 <u>Occupational exposure</u>

Airborne MMMF concentrations present in workplaces with good work practices are generally less than 1.0 fibres/ml (editor's note: corrected from IPCS). However, data reviewed indicate that mean airborne fibre levels for some workers in the ceramic fibre and small diameter (less than 1 µm) glasswool fibre manufacturing sectors may be similar to those to which workers were exposed in the early production phase. Therefore, although only a small proportion of workers are employed in these segments of the industry, their lung cancer risk could potentially be elevated. However, epidemiological data are not yet available on workers in the ceramic fibre industry. Elevated average concentrations of fibres during the blowing or spraying of insulation wool in confined spaces have also been recorded and their lung cancer risk could similarly be increased. (Editor's note: in work situations with potentially elevated airborne dust or fibre concentrations, preventive and control measures as discussed in section 6.3 should be applied.)

2.7.2 <u>Non-occupational exposure</u>

There have been isolated case reports of respiratory symptoms and dermatitis associated with exposure to MMMF in home and office environments. However, available epidemiological data are not sufficient to draw any conclusions in this respect. As with occupationally exposed populations, it is the potential risk of lung cancer at low levels of exposure that is of most concern, but no direct evidence is available from which to draw conclusions ...

However, levels of MMMF in the typical indoor and general environments measured to date, are very low compared with present levels in most sectors of the production and user industry and certainly much lower (by several orders of magnitude) than some past occupational exposure levels associated with raised lung cancer risks. It should also be noted that such increases in lung cancer risk have not been observed among workers employed under the improved conditions of the late technological phase and followed up for a sufficient length of time.

The overall picture indicates that the possible risk of lung cancer among the general public is very low, if there is any at all, and should not be a cause for concern if the current low levels of exposure continue.

Notes

[1] WHO: Man-made mineral fibres, Environmental Health Criteria 77 (Geneva, WHO, 1988).

[2] R. Klingholz: "Technology and production of man-made mineral fibres", in Annals of Occupational Hygiene, Vol. 20, 1977, pp. 153-159.

[3] B.A. Gantner: "Respiratory hazard from removal of ceramic fibre insulation from high temperature industrial furnaces", in American Industrial Hygiene Association Journal, Vol. 47, 1986, pp. 530-534.

[4] WHO: Biological effects of man-made mineral fibres, Report on a WHO/IARC meeting, Copenhagen, 20-22 Apr. 1982, EURO Reports and Studies 81 (Copenhagen, WHO Regional Office for Europe, 1983).

[5] W.H. Walton and S.M. Coppock (eds.): "Man-made mineral fibres in the working environment", in Annals of Occupational Hygiene, Vol. 31, 1987, No. 4B, pp. 517-834.

[6] WHO/IARC: Man-made mineral fibres and radon, IARC Monographs on the Evaluation of the Carcinogenic Risk of Chemicals to Humans, Vol. 43 (Lyon, International Agency for Research on Cancer, 1988).

[7] J.W. Hill: "Man-made mineral fibres", in Journal of the Society of Occupational Medicine, Vol. 28, 1978, pp. 134-141.

[8] A. Bjornberg: "Glassfibre dermatitis", in American Journal of Industrial Medicine, Vol. 8, 1985, pp. 395-400.

[9] J. Stokholm, M. Norn and T. Schneider: "Ophthalmologic effects of man-made mineral fibres", in <u>Scandinavian Journal of Work, Environment and Health</u>, Vol. 8, 1982, pp. 185–190.

3. NATURAL MINERAL FIBRES (OTHER THAN ASBESTOS)

3.1 General

A wide range of naturally occurring minerals exist in fibrous form, that is, they contain particles which conform to the occupational hygiene definition of a fibre as any particle with a length to breadth aspect ratio equal to or greater than 3:1. Included in this definition are single crystals (prismatic, acicular, filiform or bladed) and crystal aggregate patterns or arrangements (asbestiform, columnar or fibrous). Fibrous particles may also result from avulsion or cleavage of discrete particulate material.

The list of minerals containing fibrous particles is extensive and includes erionite, attapulgite and wollastonite. These are the subject of this document because of their potential for significant occupational exposure, and because they have been extensively reviewed by the International Programme on Chemical Safety (IPCS)[1] and the International Agency for Research on Cancer (IARC).[2] But there are many others, including epsomite, pectolite, pyrophyllite, anhydrite, fibrolite, zoisite, epidote, pistacite, sepiolite, halloysite, nemalite, magnesite, apjohnite, gypsum, gedrite, celestite, halotrichite and many more.

It is recognised that gypsum is very widely used, but the health effects of the fibrous particles in gypsum have not been studied. In fact, very few of the fibrous minerals have been tested in experimental systems, and there have been few studies of people exposed to them. However, the limited evidence suggests that the potential health effects differ widely. Erionite is now seen to be a potent cause of mesothelioma following low environmental exposures; attapulgite and wollastonite show limited evidence of causing pneumoconiotic changes in people occupationally exposed.

This chapter highlights the fact that many naturally occurring minerals contain fibrous particles. Employers and employees should therefore have information on the possible concentrations and properties of fibrous particles in the materials to which they are exposed, and appropriate preventive and control measures should be adopted.

3.2 Characteristics

3.2.1 Erionite

Erionite is one of the naturally occurring zeolites. Its
basic structure, like that of the other zeolites, is a framework
of alumino-silicate tetrahedra. One type of erionite occurs in a
fibrous form being made up of prismatic crystals in radiating
groups.[1]

It is believed that erionite is not currently mined or
marketed in any form for commercial purposes, but may occur as a
contaminant in some commercial zeolites. Zeolites are known to
be mined in the following 16 countries: Bulgaria, China, Cuba,
Czechoslovakia, the Federal Republic of Germany, Hungary, Italy,
Japan, Mexico, the Republic of Korea, Romania, South Africa,
Turkey, the United States, the USSR and Yugoslavia. Most of the
mining is for clinoptiolite or mordenite. World production of
natural zeolites has been estimated at 300,000 tonnes per
annum.[2]

Zeolite minerals are found as major constituents in numerous
sedimentary volcanic tuffs, especially where these were deposited
and have been altered by saline-lake water. Many hundreds of
occurrences have been recorded of zeolite deposits in over 40
countries. Erionite occurs in rocks of many types (e.g. rhyolite
tuff) and in a wide range of geological settings; however, it
rarely occurs in pure form and is normally associated with other
zeolite minerals. It is considered to have been formed by the
action of saline water on volcanic glass particles either by
percolation or immersion. Erionite occurs as deposits of
prismatic to acicular crystals several μm in length. When ground
to powder, erionite particles resemble amphibole asbestos fibres
morphologically.[2]

3.2.2 Attapulgite

Attapulgite is also known as palygorskite. Its structure is
similar to that of minerals of the amphibole group and is very
similar to sepiolite. The structural arrangement of attapulgite
results in long, thin or lath-like crystals occuring in bundles
that comprise thin sheets composed of minute interlaced fibres.[2]

Attapulgite is found in association with sepiolite,
phosphates, carbonates, opal, quartz, cristobalite, and other
clay minerals and the purity of marketed products is dependent on
the mined ore. It is known to be currently mined in the
following nine countries: Australia, France, India, Senegal,
South Africa, Spain, Turkey, the United States and the USSR. By
far the largest producer is the United States, where attapulgite
is known as "fullers' earth". Attapulgite deposits are mined by

open-pit techniques. It is then refined by conventional milling and screening techniques to produce various grades of clay products. World-wide annual production of attapulgite clays is in the order of 1.5 million tonnes.

3.2.3 Wollastonite

Wollastonite is composed of calcium oxide and silicon dioxide, although iron, magnesium or manganese may partially substitute for calcium. It occurs as coarse-bladed masses, rarely showing good crystal form. Fragments of crushed wollastonite tend to be acicular, lath-shaped or fibrous. The particle length-diameter ratios are commonly 7:1 to 8:1. Wollastonite rarely occurs in pure form, but in association with other minerals such as calcite, quartz, garnet, and diopside.[2]

At present, only nine companies world-wide are known to mine and market wollastonite. Mining is centred in the United States, where three companies operate. One company in each of the following countries also mines the mineral: Finland, India, Japan, Kenya, Mexico and New Zealand. Refinement of the ore into high-grade wollastonite is done by screening and magnetic separators. Grinding and milling operations result in variable mesh powders or aggregates. Annual world-wide production levels are in the order of 130,000 tonnes.

3.3 Occupational exposure

3.3.1 Erionite

Erionite is not mined or marketed in any form for commercial purposes. Because it can be present as a minor component in some commercial zeolites, studies of zeolite mining operations have been conducted.

Airborne dust samples were collected in an open-pit zeolite (containing erionite) mining operation in Bowie, Arizona, in 1979. Total dust exposures for labourers ranged from 0.4–5.8 mg/m^3 (eight samples); concentrations in the mining area were 0.01–13.7 mg/m^3 (nine samples). Respirable dust concentrations in the mining area ranged from 0.01–1.4 mg/m^3 (five samples). Airborne dust concentrations of quartz and cristobalite were below the limits of detection (0.03 mg for 100–800 litre air samples). Analyses of airborne and bulk samples by electron microscopy did not suggest substantial exposure to fibres.[3]

Rock samples from a zeolite deposit in Rome, Oregon, contained numerous fibres 0.02–0.5 μm in diameter and 0.5–60 μm in length. Fibrous material made up 10–30 per cent and 8–20 per cent of two samples taken from one erionite zone of the deposit, while the content of fibres in a sample from another area was less than 1 per cent. No data on occupational exposure were available, since the deposit was not being actively mined.[4]

3.3.2 Attapulgite

Attapulgite, as a component of various naturally occurring clays, was probably used in ancient times in pottery, and for removing oil in cloth manufacture. Currently, the main uses for attapulgite are in pet waste absorbents, oil and grease absorbents, drilling muds, pesticides and related products, fertilisers and cosmetics, and pharmaceutical products. It has been shown that attapulgite fibres can absorb polyaromatic hydrocarbons such as benzo-a-pyrene.[5]

In 1976 about 200 dust samples were collected at various milling operations in a United States attapulgite production plant. During crushing, milling, drying and screening, the average concentrations in the workers' breathing zone ranged from 0.05 to 2.1 mg/m^3 for total dust and from 0.02 to 0.32 mg/m^3 for respirable dust. Except for some individual samples, respirable free silica exposures calculated for each job category were below 0.05 mg/m^3. As determined by transmission electron microscopy, airborne attapulgite fibres had a count median diameter of 0.07 µm and a median length of 0.4 µm, with ranges of 0.02 to 0.1 µm in diameter and 0.1 to 2.5 µm in length.[6]

Dust concentrations were measured in several hundred air samples in two United States companies mining and milling attapulgite clay. The mean concentration of total dust ranged from 0.6 to 3.1 mg/m^3 in mining and from 0.1 to 23 mg/m^3 in milling and shipping operations. On average, the concentration of respirable dust was below 5 mg/m^3 in all job categories.[2]

There are no available data on occupational dust exposures in the user industries.

3.3.3 Wollastonite

Wollastonite was probably first mined in the 1930s for mineral wool production, but significant commercial production did not commence until about 1950. Since then wollastonite has become widely used, especially in the ceramics industry. The other main areas of use are in paints, plastics and rubber, abrasives and in metallurgy.

The IARC has described the uses of wollastonite in the following terms:[2]

Ceramics. Wollastonite is used in some ceramic products, and this use accounts for over half of its consumption world-wide. Wollastonite has several advantages over more typical ceramic raw materials, the most notable being faster firing time. Ceramic materials have included up to 70 per cent w/w wollastonite, and published recipes for ceramic tiles have included 5, 8, 36, 55 and 67 per cent wollastonite, in combination with clays, flint and talc. Other ceramics applications include glazes and fluxes, ceramic artware and dinnerware, and electrical insulating materials.

Paints and coatings. Wollastonite is used as an extender in both oil- and water-based emulsion paints for exterior use, and in latex and road-marking paints. Because of the brilliant nature of its white colour (when very pure), its low oil absorption, high pH and good wetting abilities, it is added to many types of coatings, where it imparts colour, fluidity and mildew-resistance. Paint-grade wollastonite, a fine high-purity grade, has been added at levels of 9-13 per cent w/w to many paints in the United States.

Plastics and rubber. Wollastonite has been incorporated as a filler in plastics because of its colour and structural properties and has been used in epoxy resins as a 50 per cent loading pigment.

Other uses. A current and increasing use of wollastonite is as a replacement for asbestos. Coarser grades of wollastonite are used at up to 50 per cent with other fillers, binders and organic fibres for heat-containment panels. It has also been used for ceiling and floor tiling, brake linings and high-temperature appliances.

An important European application of natural and synthetic wollastonite is in welding powders and fluxes for metal casting. The strucural properties of wollastonite render fluxes useful for insulating molten materials before cooling.

Wollastonite has also been used in abrasives, in welding electrodes, as a soil conditioner and plant fertiliser, as a substitute for limestone and sand in glass manufacture, as a filler in paper and as a road material.

According to the same source, airborne dust and fibre concentrations have been measured in the two largest wollastonite production plants in the world:

The Finnish quarry produced wollastonite as a side-product of limestone mining. Consequently, the operational stages from drilling in the open cast mine to fine crushing before froth flotation processing at a separate location, involved mixed exposures to wollastonite fibres and granular calcite dust. On average, the quarried stone contained about 15 per cent wollastonite and 2-3 per cent quartz. A similar mean composition was also found for the respirable fraction of dust samples from mining and milling operations. In drilling, crushing and sorting, the concentration of total dust ranged from 2 to 99 mg/m^3 and the levels of airborne fibres from 1 to 45 f/ml, as measured by phase-contrast optical microscopy. In the flotation and bagging plant, dust was mainly composed of wollastonite, and workplace concentrations ranged from 15 to 30 mg/m^3 for total dust and from 8 to 37 f/ml for fibres, as counted by phase-contrast optical microscopy. In all operations, the mean level of respirable quartz was below 0.1 mg/m^3. The counting criteria were the same as those most commonly used for asbestos: all fibres over 5 μm in length, less than 3 um in diameter and with an aspect ratio over 3:1 were counted. When studied by scanning electron microscopy, the thinnest wollastonite fibres were characteristically 0.2-0.3 μm in diameter. The median fibre lengths and median diameter were 4 μm and 0.8 μm in crushing operations and 2 μm and 0.4 μm in bagging work.

Similar results have been reported from the United States wollastonite production plant. In open-cast and underground mining, crushing, packing and maintenance, the mean concentration of total dust ranged from 0.9 to 10 mg/m^3. Bulk samples contained less than 2 per cent free silica, and respirable silica concentrations ranged from less than 0.01 to 0.13 mg/m^3. In the same operations, airborne fibre counts by phase-contrast optical microscopy showed a mean of 0.3 f/ml in the mine and a range of 0.8-8.48 f/ml in the mill. Fibrous particles had a median diameter of 0.22 μm and a median length of 2.5 μm.

The only available data on occupational exposures during the use of wollastonite refer to its use in the production of fibre-reinforced cement sheets. Airborne fibre levels ranging from 0.02 to 0.2 f/ml have been measured during stacking and mixing.[2]

3.4   Non-occupational exposure

3.4.1   Erionite

All the human health effects outlined in paragraph 3.5.1 relate to community exposures in Turkey. Erionite fibres have been found in soil samples from an agricultural area in Central Cappadocia, Turkey. Rock and dust samples from the villages of Tuzkoy and Karain contained fibres less than 0.25 μm in diameter and more than 5 μm in length, with elemental ratios consistent with erionite.[7]

Airborne fibre levels have also been measured in Karain and another village in Turkey, Karlik, using transmission electron microscopy. Concentrations of fibres greater than 5 μm in length were below 0.01 f/ml in the streets of both villages (20 samples), whereas concentrations in some work and recreational areas in Karain (stone cutting, fields during agricultural activity, schoolyard) ranged from 0.2-0.3 f/ml. All indoor samples taken in Karlik contained less than 0.01 f/ml whereas seven of the 11 indoor samples taken from Karain contained 0.03-1.38 f/ml. Approximately 80 per cent of respirable fibres in Karain and 20 per cent in Karlik had chemical compositions similar to those of erionite, the rest consisting mainly of calcite.[8]

3.4.2 Attapulgite

Hundreds of thousands of people are exposed to attapulgite when used as pet litter in homes, but no reports of dust levels or possible health effects are available.

3.4.3 Wollastonite

There are no available data on non-occupational exposure to wollastonite dusts, nor on their possible effects on health.

3.5 Health effects

3.5.1 Erionite

The IARC[2] has concluded in its overall evaluation of the health effects of erionite that there is sufficient evidence of the carcinogenicity of erionite in experimental animals and in humans. Erionite is listed by the IARC in Group 1.

The evidence for health effects in people has come from observations in residents of regions of Turkey where erionite deposits occur.[9] Studies have demonstrated very high mortality from malignant mesothelioma, mainly of the pleura, in three Turkish villages. There was soil and rock contamination with erionite, and villagers' exposure was from birth. Erionite fibres were identified in lung tissue samples in cases of pleural mesothelioma, and ferruginous bodies were found in the sputum in a much higher proportion of inhabitants in contaminated villages than in control groups.

In experimental systems fibrous erionite was tested in rats by inhalation and by intrapleural administration, and in mice by intraperitoneal injection. All the tests resulted in high incidences of mesotheliomas by all routes of administration. Although mesothelioma was the most serious outcome, the initial reaction was widespread tissue inflamation leading to severe fibrosis.

3.5.2 Attapulgite

The health effects of attapulgite have also been reviewed by the IARC[2] which has concluded that there is limited evidence of the carcinogenicity of attapulgite in experimental animals and inadequate evidence of its carcinogenicity in humans. Attapulgite is listed by the IARC in Group 3.

Surveys of attapulgite workers have been carried out. Radiographs and pulmonary function measurements of 701 workers, taken in the course of routine surveillance by two companies in the United States, were analysed. The workers were employed in mining and milling of attapulgite clay. The overall prevalence of pneumoconiosis (profusion greater than 1/0 in the ILO International Classification of Radiographs of Pneumoconioses, 1980) was 6.4 per cent. The prevalence of radiographical changes increased consistently (but not statistically significantly) with age and with cumulative exposure to dust. The prevalence of pneumoconiosis among workers exposed for more than 15 years was 11.9 per cent in one company and 25.3 per cent in the other, after allowing for age, race and smoking habits. Lung function was reduced among workers in one company.

A single epidemiological study of attapulgite miners and millers showed increased mortality from lung cancer among a small group with long-term, high-level exposure. But there were many deficiencies in the epidemiological methods and a causal link between attapulgite and lung cancer could not be established.

In experimental systems, attapulgite samples from different deposits were tested for carcinogenicity in rats in one experiment by intraperitoneal injection, and in two experiments by intrapleural application. An attapulgite sample with 30 per cent of fibres longer than 5 µm produced mesotheliomas and sarcomas in the abdominal cavity following intraperitoneal injection. In addition, one sample of attapulgite with less than 2 per cent of fibres longer than 4 µm was reported to induce mesothelial tumours following intrapleural administration. Two samples of another attapulgite with less than 1 per cent of fibres longer than 4 µm did not cause a significant increase in the incidence of tumours following intrapleural administration.

8611d

3.5.3 Wollastonite

The health effects of wollastonite have also been reviewed by the IARC.[2] It has concluded that there is limited evidence of the carcinogenicity of wollastonite in experimental animals and inadequate evidence of its carcinogenicity in humans. Wollastonite is listed by the IARC in Group 3.

One small study of wollastonite quarry workers in Finland has demonstrated mild parenchymal and pleural changes in the lungs. In the United States, surveys at a wollastonite mine and mill revealed the prevalence of pneumoconiosis (profusion greater than 1/0 in the ILO International Classification of Radiographs of Pneumoconioses, 1980) as four cases among 76 miners and three cases among 108 millers in 1982. Lung function tests suggested a mild dust-related limitation of air flow. No pleural changes were noted.

There has been only one epidemiological study of the possible carcinogenic effects of wollastonite. In Finland a mortality study of 192 male and 46 female workers who had worked at a limestone-wollastonite quarry for at least one year was carried out. One rare mesenchymal tumour of the retroperitoneum occurred 30 years after first exposure in a non-smoking woman who had held various production jobs in the quarry for 16 years. Her occupational history did not reveal any other dust exposure. Apart from this one rare tumour, there was no evidence of an excess of cancer.

In experimental systems four grades of wollastonite of different particle sizes were tested for carcinogenicity in one experiment in rats by intrapleural implantation. A significant increase in the incidence of pleural sarcomas was observed with two grades, and a statistically non-significant increase with a third grade, all of which contained fibres greater than 4 μm in length and less than 0.5 μm in diameter. Pleural sarcomas were not observed after implantation of the grade that contained relatively few fibres with these dimensions.

3.5.4 Summary of health effects

The evidence from the villagers in Turkey demonstrates clearly that erionite can cause mesothelioma from low fibre exposures. The carcinogenic properties of erionite have also been well demonstrated by tests in experimental animals.

There is no clear evidence that attapulgite and wollastonite cause cancer in humans; but the results of small prevalence studies suggest that these dusts can cause pneumoconiotic changes. Animal experiments provided limited evidence for carcinogenicity of both minerals.

8611d

Notes

[1] WHO: Asbestos and other natural mineral fibres, Environmental Health Criteria 53 (Geneva, WHO, 1986).

[2] WHO/IARC: Silica and some silicates, IARC Monographs on the Evaluation of the Carcinogenic Risk of Chemicals to Humans, No. 42 (Lyon, International Agency for Research on Cancer, 1987).

[3] W.C. Roberts, G.R. Rapp and J.L. Webber: Encyclopaedia of minerals, (New York, Van Norstrand Reinhold, 1974).

[4] R.F. Herrick and C. Robinson: Survey report on zeolite ore mining near Bowie, Arizona, NIOSH Report No. 111.10; Report No. PB81-241689 (Cincinnati, National Institute for Occupational Safety and Health, 1981).

[5] G. Harvey, M. Page and L. Dumas: "Binding of environmental carcinogens to asbestos and mineral fibres", in British Journal of Industrial Medicine, Vol. 41, 1984, pp. 396-400.

[6] A. Albers: Mining environmental target investigation: Natural zeolites (Morgantown, National Institute for Occupational Safety and Health, 1981).

[7] R. Zumwalde: Industrial hygiene study: Engelhard Minerals and Chemicals Corporation, Attapulgus, Georgia (NIOSH 00106935) (Cincinnati, National Institute for Occupational Safety and Health, 1976).

[8] F.D. Pooley: "Evaluation of fibre samples taken from the vicinity of two villages in Turkey", in R. Lemen and J.H. Dement (eds.): Dusts and disease (Park Forest South, Illinois, Pathotox, 1979).

[9] Y.I. Baris, R. Saracci, L. Simonato, J.W. Skidmore and M. Artivinli: "Malignant mesothelioma and radiological chest abnormalities in two villages in central Turkey: An epidemiological and environmental investigation", in Lancet, Vol. 1, 1981, pp. 984-987.

4. SYNTHETIC ORGANIC FIBRES

4.1 General

Synthetic fibres are made from polymers that have been synthetically produced from chemical elements or compounds obtained from the petrochemical industry. The following are the main groups of substances from which the fibres are produced: polyamides, polyesters, polyvinyl derivatives, polyolefins, polyurethanes and polytetrafluoroethylenes.[1] The most common generic and trade names of the products are summarised in table 2.

Most of the synthetic organic fibres are used in the textile industry. More recently some synthetic organic fibres have been developed with improved properties such as durability, strength and resistance to chemicals. When manufactured to fine diameters, some of these products have excellent insulation and heat resistance properties, and because of this they are being used more extensively instead of natural and man-made mineral fibres. The principal types are aramid fibres, carbon/graphite fibres and polyolefin fibres. The first and the third are organic polymers, whilst carbon/graphite fibres consist predominantly of carbon. This chapter deals with these three groups of fibres, not with those used in the textile industry.

Although most of the fibres are made to nominal diameters much greater than the respirable diameter (3 μm), the potential still exists for occupational exposures to respirable fibres and to respirable dust particles. Because of the durability of the products, and because one of the aramid fibres has demonstrated fibrogenic and carcinogenic effects in experimental animals, it is important that these substances are regarded with caution. Systems and standards should be developed to ensure safety in their manufacture and use.

It is important to note that a number of the raw materials and intermediate products in the manufacturing of synthetic organic fibres may have toxic properties. The same is true for the products of the thermal decomposition of the fibres. These aspects, as well as the control of exposure of workers and the protection of their health against harmful effects of such chemicals, are not covered here. This document deals with the health effects of the inhaled fibres.

Table 2.   Generic and trade names of selected
           synthetic organic fibres

Polyamides	Nylon 66 (United States, United Kingdom), Anid (Spain), Ducilo (Argentina), Nailon (Italy), Nylsuisse (Switzerland), Perlon T (Federal Republic of Germany); Nylon 6 (United States), Amilon (Japan), Dayan (Spain), Kapron (USSR), Lilion (Italy), Perlon, Kevlar and Twaron (Federal Republic of Germany, United States).
Polyesters	Dacron (United States), Diolen (Federal Republic of Germany), Lavsan (USSR), Tergal (France), Terital and Wistel (Italy), Terylene (United Kingdom), Tetoron (Japan), Trevira (Federal Republic of Germany), Nigerlene (Nigeria).
Polyacrylonitrile	Acrilon and Orlon (United States), Amlana (Poland), Courtelle (United Kingdom), Crylor (France), Leacril and Velicren (Italy), Dolan (Federal Republic of Germany, United Kingdom).
Polyolefins	Courlene Pulpex and Ulstron (United Kingdom), Hostalen (Federal Republic of Germany), Meraklon (Italy).
Polyurethane	Lycra, Glospan and Vyrene (United States), Spandell (United Kingdom), Dorlestan and Lycra (Federal Republic of Germany).
Polytetrafluoroethylene	Teflon.

Source: Adapted from ILO: Encyclopaedia of occupational health
         and safety (Geneva, 1983).

Among the variety of synthetic organic fibres, the three materials, aramid fibres, carbon and graphite fibres, and polyolefin fibres, have been selected because of their potential for generating airborne respirable fibres, and because of the availability of information on them.   It is important to point out that there has been no evaluation of their health effects by either the International Programme for Chemical Safety (IPCS) or by the International Agency for Research on Cancer (IARC).

4.2 Characteristics

4.2.1 Aramid fibres

Aramid fibres are products formed from a long chain polyamide.[2] There are currently two types of aramid fibre in world production. The first, para-aramid, is composed of a polymer of p-phenylenediamine and terephthaloyl chloride. It is manufactured in the United States and Ireland under the trademark Kevlar[R], and in the Netherlands under the trademark Twaron[R]. The second type, meta-aramid, is composed of a polymer of m-phenylenediamine and isophthaloyl chloride. It is manufactured in the United States under the trademark Nomex[R], and in Japan under the trademark Teijinconex[R].

The two aramid types are both manufactured to diameters of approximately 12 μm. The polymer is prepared in solution, spun, and then extruded through spinnerets. Both types have high tensile strength, are resistant to heat, flame and most chemicals, and are good electrical insulators, but the first type, Kevlar[R]/Twaron[R], is very much stronger. The other very important difference is that the first type can generate fine fibres of less than 1 μm diameter.

Kevlar[R]/Twaron[R] is manufactured as continuous multi-filament yarn, cut fibre (staple), staple yarn, fabrics, and pulp. Pulp is made of strands chopped to lengths of 2-8 mm. The chopping process generates fine fibres known by the manufacturers as "fibrils", and the pulp manufacturing process strives to produce a fibrillated surface as this enhances the usefulness of the product. The fine fibres are of a diameter of more than 0.1 μm and 3 to 1,000 μm long. Both the mixing and reinforcing properties of the product are improved by the fine fibres because of their great length to breadth ratio.

Staple production results in strands of 3 to 80 mm length. In the process, fine fibres are also generated by the chopping action but not intentionally by the process.

Nomex[R]/Teijinconex[R] is manufactured as continuous filament, and is also cut into staple fibre. It is not made as pulp. The products are all made to a diameter of 12 μm. A proportion of the production output is converted into paper by the manufacturer. This involves the production of flakes. Fine fibres are not produced in fibre and paper production or use.

4.2.2 Carbon and graphite fibres

Although carbon is an element, carbon and graphite fibres are dealt with in the chapter of synthetic organic fibres in view of the production of carbon and graphite fibres predominantly from organic compounds. They are made by high temperature processing (carbonisation) of one of three precursor materials: rayon (regenerated cellulose), pitch (coal tar or petroleum residue), or polyacrylonitrile (PAN). PAN-based carbon fibres are the most common.

The terms "carbon" and "graphite" are often used interchangeably, but there are differences. Graphite fibres require higher temperatures for their production, usually 2000-3000°C, compared with carbon fibres which are manufactured at about 1300°C. Graphite fibres are stronger and stiffer than carbon fibres. The main producers of carbon and graphite fibres are Japan, the United States and the United Kingdom. Japan is the leading producer of PAN-based fibres, and the United States is the leader in rayon and pitch-based fibres.

These fibres are characterised by light weight, high tensile strength, flexibility, good electrical conductivity, thermal resistance and chemical inertness. They are manufactured to nominal diameters of 5 to 8 μm, but up to 25 per cent of the product may be of less than 3 μm in diameter and less than 80 μm in length. After mechanical or thermal stress, carbon and graphite fibres may break into finer respirable particles.

4.2.3 Polyolefin fibres

Polyolefin fibres are made from polymers of ethylene, propylene, or other olefin units. About 95 per cent of these fibres are made from polypropylene.[3]

The fibres are manufactured as monofilament yarn with diameters of more than 150 μm, multifilament yarn with each filament of 5 to 20 μm, tape and yarn as a continuous sheet, spunbonded fabric, chopped multifilament (staple), synthetic pulp with diameters of 5 to 40 μm and length of 2.5 to 3.0 mm and microfibre with diameters of 1.0 to 5.0 um. They do not split longitudinally to form finer fibres.

4.3 Occupational exposure

4.3.1 Aramid fibres

Airborne respirable fibre levels have been measured during manufacture of Kevlar[R]/Twaron[R] staple and range from less than 0.01 f/ml to 0.4 f/ml in staple making (unpublished industry data).

Kevlar[R]/Twaron[R] fibres are used for tyre cords, protective clothing, including bullet-proof clothing, heat and fire-resistant clothing, industrial fabrics, high performance composites, high strength ropes and cables, and friction materials.

The user exposures of most concern are those where the product is used either in the pulp form to make friction materials or the staple form to spin yarn. Pulp is usually supplied in bags in a dry form (4-8 per cent moisture), and is mixed with other materials after "fluffing" to release the fibres. The final products include disc brake pads, brake blocks for heavy vehicles, and other industrial friction materials. Airborne respirable fibre levels have been measured at plants using dry pulp. The results range from less than 0.01 f/ml to 0.09 f/ml. Spinning of yarn from staple for use in protective clothing, clutch linings and other applications can also produce respirable fibres. Airborne respirable fibre levels have been measured and found to range up to 2.9 f/ml, most values being between 0.2 and 0.9 f/ml (unpublished industry data). The other uses of Kevlar[R]/Twaron[R] are not associated with the potential for release of respirable fibres. Also, processes which abrade Kevlar[R]/Twaron[R] continuous filament yarn, such as weaving or machining, may also generate respirable fibres. Airborne respirable fibre levels have been found up to 0.3 f/ml (unpublished industry data).

Nomex[R]/Teijinconex[R] is produced as paper, staple, or continuous filament yarn. The major use for the paper is as electrical insulation in motors and transformers. The major uses for staple and continuous filament are industrial filter bags for hot gas emissions; protective clothing; and coated fabrics. This type of aramid fibre is not manufactured in fibres of respirable diameter, and such fibres are not produced during use. Monitoring for airborne respirable fibres has been carried out, with all results less than 0.01 f/ml which was the limit of detection (unpublished industry data).

4.3.2 Carbon and graphite fibres

Carbon and graphite fibres have a wide range of uses because of their properties of high mechanical strength and elasticity, low density and high heat and chemical resistance. They are mainly used as reinforcing materials in structural composites and in high temperature insulation applications.

These fibres are made to nominal diameters of 5 to 8 μm, with up to 25 per cent of the product having a diameter of less than 3 μm. Additionally, they may break during processing to generate respirable dust particles. Results of airborne respirable fibre monitoring are not available, but dust concentrations have been reported in manufacturing plants in the United Kingdom[4] and the USSR.[5] In the former, the mean levels for the dustiest group (laboratory workers) were 0.39

mg/m^3 total dust and 0.16 mg/m^3 respirable dust. In the USSR study, total dust concentrations were found to be currently in the range of 0.3 to 5.7 mg/m^3; however, in individual operations, the total dust concentrations exceeded 15 mg/m^3.

4.3.3 Polyolefin fibres

Polyolefin fibres have been very widely used for decades, particularly in carpets and rugs, and in home furnishings such as upholstery, curtains and bedding. A more recent innovation is the use of fine polypropylene fibres (1-5 μm diameter) in the manufacture of lightweight, moisture-resistant, insulating clothing. Examples of this use are divers' suits, sportswear, gloves and bedding.

Apart from the recent use of fine fibres, polyolefins are mostly large diameter fibres, and the potential for airborne respirable fibres has not been considered a problem. No data on airborne dust or fibre levels are available to support this.

4.4 Non-occupational exposure

There are no available data on non-occupational exposures to synthetic organic fibres nor on their possible effects on health.

4.5 Health effects

4.5.1 Aramid fibres

There is no available information on adverse health effects of aramid fibres in humans.

Animal experiments have been conducted in which rats inhaled ultrafine Kevlar^R fibres (para-aramid) of defined sizes (mostly less than 1.0 μm diameter and 10 to 30 μm length) for two weeks.[6] The authors reported mild to moderate foreign body reaction at concentrations of 3 mg/m^3 (280 f/ml) and 18 mg/m^3 (about 2000 f/ml). Fibrosis was seen at the 18 mg/m^3 exposure and remained after exposure. There were no adverse effects seen at < 0.5 mg/m^3.

There has also been one chronic inhalation study of two years' duration.[7] Rats were exposed to ultrafine Kevlar^R fibres with diameters mostly less than 1.5 μm and lengths of less than 20 μm at concentrations of 2.5, 25, 100 and 400 f/ml. The authors reported that the highest exposure group showed severe lung damage after one year and dust exposures were ceased. Cystic keratinising squamous cell tumours were found in the rats exposed to the two highest dose levels. Additionally, dose-dependent fibrosis was found in rats exposed to 25, 100, and 400 f/ml. No adverse effects were found at the 2.5 f/ml exposure level.

The effects of Kevlar[R] have also been studied by injecting fibres into the peritoneal cavity of rats.[8,9] The authors reported a mild level of fibrosis, and also a weak carcinogenic effect. The incidence of mesotheliomas was 6 to 13 per cent but was not dose-related. The fibres were less than 1.0 um in diameter.

The Nomex[R] type of meta-aramid fibre has not been shown to cause the adverse effects, associated with the exposure to the fine (diameter less than 1.5 um) para-aramid fibres.

4.5.2 Carbon and graphite fibres

In one study of health effects of 88 people employed in PAN-based carbon fibre manufacture,[4] the authors concluded that there were no ill effects of carbon fibre on the lungs of those working in the production unit. Dust concentrations were low, with mean levels for the dustiest (laboratory) group being 0.39 mg/m^3 total dust, and 0.16 mg/m^3 respirable dust. The carbon fibres 8-10 μm in diameter fractured laterally but not longitudinally into fine fibres. Respirable particles were mostly non-fibrous and were composed of resin and extraneous material.

In another study, 162 workers from the production of carbon fibres (exposed to concentrations referred to in section 4.2.2) were examined. The author reported that respiratory function deterioration was found in 42 per cent of them, and incipient atrophic changes of the mucosa of the upper respiratory tract in almost half of them.[5]

There have been several acute and subchronic inhalation studies in experimental animals. With the exception of one, none of the studies has shown any evidence of lung cancers or fibrosis. The authors of one study, however,[10] reported fibrosis following intratracheal installation of carbon fibres. In the same study, chrysotile asbestos was shown to be many times more fibrogenic than the carbon fibre.

4.5.3 Polyolefin fibres

There is no available information on health effects of polyolefin fibres in humans. Experimental animal studies are limited to injection studies only and no clear evidence of an adverse health effect has been reported. There have been no inhalation studies.

4.5.4 Summary of health effects

There is evidence that Kevlar[R] aramid fibres can cause fibrosis and lung tumours in inhalation exposure studies on rats.

There is one report on lung function deterioration in workers producing carbon fibres.

There are no data available on the health effects of polyolefin fibres.

Notes

[1] ILO: Encyclopaedia of Occupational Health and Safety (Geneva, 1983).

[2] J. Preston: "Aramid fibres", in Kirk-Othmer Encyclopaedia of Chemical Technology, Vol. 3 (New York, John Wiley and Sons, 1979).

[3] D.R. Buchanan: "Olefin fibres", in Kirk-Othmer Encyclopaedia of Chemical Technology, Vol. 16, op. cit.

[4] H.D. Jones, T.R. Jones and W.H. Lyle: "Carbon fibre: Results of a survey of process workers and their environment in a factory producing continuous filament", in Annals of Occupational Hygiene, Vol. 26, 1982, pp. 861-868.

[5] R.P. Fedjakina: "Occupational hygiene in the production of carbon fibrous materials on the basis of polyacrylonitrile and hydratecellulose fibres", in Gigiena Truda i Professionalnye Zabolevanija, 1985, No. 9, pp. 26-29 (in Russian).

[6] K.P. Lee, D.P. Kelly and G.L. Kennedy, Jr.: "Pulmonary response to inhaled Kevlar[R] aramid synthetic fibres in rats", in Toxicology and Applied Pharmacology, Vol. 71, 1983, pp. 242-253.

[7] K.P. Lee, D.P. Kelly, F.O. O'Neal, J.C. Stadler and G.L. Kennedy, Jr.: "Lung response to ultrafine Kevlar[R] aramid synthetic fibrils following a two-year inhalation exposure in rats", in Fundamental and Applied Toxicology, Vol. 11, 1988, pp. 1-20.

[8] J.M.G. Davis: Carcinogenicity of Kevlar[R] aramid pulp following intraperitoneal injection into rats, Report No. TM/87/12 (Edinburgh, Institute of Occupational Medicine, 1987).

[9] F. Pott, M. Roller, U. Ziem, F.-J. Reiffer, B. Bellmann, M. Rosenbruch and F. Huth: Carcinogenicity studies on natural

and man-made fibres with the intraperitoneal test in rats, paper presented at the IARC Symposium on Mineral Fibres in the Non-Occupational Environment, Lyon, 8-10 Sep. 1987.

[10] N.A. Troickaja, B.T. Velichkovskij, F.M. Kogan and L.N. El'nichnykh: "Comparative fibrogenicity of carbon fibres and asbestos", in Gigiena i Sanitarija, 1984, Vol. 6, pp. 18-20 (in Russian).

5. MONITORING OF AIRBORNE DUST IN THE WORKING ENVIRONMENT

5.1 General

The following methods are used for measuring concentrations of the total airborne dusts or respirable fibres in the working environment.

5.2 Gravimetric determination of airborne dusts

There are no specific gravimetric methods for dusts containing mineral fibres, whether natural or man-made, but the following general methods are available.

The ILO refers to a gravimetric method of measuring airborne dust containing asbestos fibres, the principles of which can be applied to any type of mineral fibres.[1] It uses high-volume sampling and is intended for area sampling, not for personal sampling.

Several gravimetric methods are available[2,3,4] for personal (breathing zone) sampling. The methods sample dust of particle sizes conforming approximately to the definitions for inspirable or total inhalable dust.[5,6] In general terms, these definitions refer to airborne particles taken in through the nose or mouth during breathing.

5.3 Determination of airborne respirable fibre concentrations

The ILO,[1] WHO/EURO[7] and NIOSH[8] provide methods for measuring airborne respirable fibres based on the widely used membrane filter method.

The ILO code of practice, Safety in the use of asbestos,[1] states the principles for air sampling and determination of airborne asbestos fibre concentrations by optical microscopy and refers to the Asbestos International Association's Membrane Filter Method for more detail. The WHO/EURO reference method and the NIOSH method are described in more detail.

The methods differ in the following respects, which can influence the results of the evaluation of the dust concentrations:

Table 3. Determination of airborne respirable fibre concentrations. Main characteristics of the methods proposed by the ILO, WHO/EURO and NIOSH

ILO	WHO/EURO	NIOSH
Flow rate		
Sample flow rate of 1 l/min ± 5% specified.	Flow rate between 0.5 and 2 l/min allowed (to optimise filter loading).	Flow above 0.5 l/min, normally 2 l/min; lower if dusty, higher if clean air.
Counting and sizing fibres		
Only respirable fibres are counted, i.e. those with a diameter of less than 3 um and a length greater than 5 um, and a length to diameter ratio greater than 3:1.	Both respirable and non-respirable fibres are counted.	Fibres with a length greater than 5 um, less than 3 um in diameter, and a length to diameter ratio equal or greater than 5:1 are counted.
All fibres or their agglomerates must be less than 3 um in diameter over their full length.	Fibres are counted as respirable if the "average" diameter is less than 3 um, and regardless of particles attached to fibres.	At least 200 fibre ends must be counted, divided by 2 to give the number of fibres (or the number in 100 graticule fields, if fewer).
At least 100 fibres must be counted with a minimum of 20 graticule areas examined.	100 graticule areas are counted unless more than 100 fibres are observed. Minimum of 20 graticule areas must be evaluated.	A minimum of 20 graticule fields must be examined.
Detection limit		
Detection limit is specified as 0.1 fibre/ml.	A detection level of 0.05 fibre/ml can normally be achieved without difficulty. Lower detection levels may be possible.	0.04 fibre/ml for 8 h sample and 2 l/min; 0.02 to 1.25 fibre/ml under other conditions.

44

8611d

5.4 Determination of airborne synthetic organic fibres

For the measurement of concentrations of airborne synthetic organic fibres, the gravimetric methods for environmental monitoring of exposure to vegetable dust have been used. The principles of such methods have been reviewed by the WHO.[9]

The total dust can be assessed by electrostatic precipitators, high-volume samplers with cellulose or fibre-glass filters, or gravimetric dust samplers. Several types of samplers using elutriator or cyclone-type size-preselectors have been used for size-selective sampling of vegetable fibre dust. This permits the separation of the respirable fraction of less than 7 µm aerodynamic diameter from the coarser inhalable dust.

Notes

[1] ILO: Safety in the use of asbestos, in ILO code of practice (Geneva, 1984).

[2] Health and Safety Executive: General methods for the gravimetric determination of respirable and total inhalable dust, MDHS14 (London, Her Majesty's Stationery Office, 1986).

[3] D. Mark and J.H. Vincent: "A new personal sampler for airborne total dust in workplaces", in Annals of Occupational Hygiene, 1986, Vol. 30, pp. 89-102.

[4] H.J. Beaulieu, A.V. Fidino, K.L.B. Arlington and R.M. Buchan: "A comparison of aerosol sampling techniques: Open versus closed-face filter cassettes", in American Industrial Hygiene Association Journal, 1980, Vol. 41, pp. 758-765.

[5] International Standards Organisation (ISO): Air quality - Particle size fraction definitions in health-related sampling, Technical Report ISO/TR 7708 (Geneva, 1983).

[6] R.F. Phalen, W.C. Hinds, W. John, T.J. Lioy, M. Lippmann, M.A. McCawley, B.J. Raabe, S.C. Soderholm and B.O. Stuart: "Rationale and recommendations for particle size - Selective sampling in the workplace", in Applied Industrial Hygiene, 1986, Vol. 1, pp. 3-14.

[7] WHO: "Reference methods for measuring airborne man-made mineral fibres (MMMF)", in Environmental Health 4 (Copenhagen, WHO Regional Office for Europe, 1985).

[8] NIOSH: NIOSH Method 7400, Revision 1:5/15/85.

[9] WHO: Recommended health-based exposure limits for selected vegetable dusts, Technical Report Series 684 (Geneva, 1983).

8611d

6. PREVENTIVE AND CONTROL MEASURES

6.1 General ILO principles

The ILO has formulated in its Conventions and Recommendations and codes of practice general principles for the protection of the health of workers against harmful agents at work, which should be applied also in work with natural and synthetic fibres. It is good industrial practice to apply these general principles for the control of any environment where dust emissions may occur.

This chapter summarises the provisions of the most general ILO international instruments on the subject and draws attention to specific considerations relating to the use of mineral and synthetic fibres.

6.1.1 International labour instruments relating to occupational safety and health

The most general ILO instruments cover nearly all aspects of occupational health and safety and are applicable to all branches of economic activity and all types of work. The most important are the Occupational Safety and Health Convention, 1981 (No. 155), and Recommendation (No. 164), which provide for the formulation and implementation of a coherent national policy on occupational safety and health and the working environment. The Working Environment (Air Pollution, Noise and Vibration) Convention, 1977 (No. 148), and Recommendation (No. 156) and the Occupational Cancer Convention, 1974 (No. 139), and Recommendation (No. 147) provide for measures to be taken for the prevention and control of, and protection against, occupational hazards in the working environment arising from exposure to the agents referred to. The Occupational Health Services Convention, 1985 (No. 161), and Recommendation (No. 171) describe the functions of these services.

The principles on which the most general instruments are based can be summarised as follows.

The field of application covers all branches of economic activity. Exclusions are permitted after consultation with the most representative organisations of employers and workers. The instruments provide that all workers should benefit from their application, and consideration shall be given to the possibility of including self-employed persons and workers in the informal sector in the full coverage of the provisions.

The instruments describe actions to be taken at the national and enterprise levels and indicate the respective roles of the competent authority, employers and workers and their organisations.

The member States shall, in the light of national conditions and practice, and in consultation with the most representative organisations of employers and workers, formulate, implement and periodically review a coherent national policy on occupational safety and health and the working environment. The policy shall aim at preventing occupational accidents and diseases by minimising, so far as is reasonably practicable, the causes of hazards inherent in the working environment.

At the national level, this policy shall be implemented by a number of activities:

- national laws or regulations shall prescribe that measures be taken for the prevention and control of, and protection against, occupational hazards in the working environment;

- the measures prescribed by national laws or regulations shall cover such elements as design, construction and layout of undertakings, work processes and substances or agents to which workers may be exposed, as well as appropriate control measures;

- exposure limits, such as maximum allowable concentrations of harmful substances in the air, limits for levels of noise or radiation, shall be specified where appropriate;

- prohibition, limitation or authorisation of certain work processes or uses of certain substances shall be considered, as appropriate;

- procedures for the notification of occupational accidents and diseases shall be established and applied, and the data statistically analysed.

An appropriate inspection system shall secure the enforcement of laws and regulations. Education and training in occupational safety and appropriate work practices should be provided.

At the level of the undertaking, the employers shall be required to:

- ensure that, so far as is reasonably practicable, the workplaces, machinery, equipment and processes under their control are safe and without risk to workers' health;

- provide workers with appropriate personal protective equipment when necessary; however, as far as possible, the working environment shall be primarily kept free from any hazard by technical measures;

- apply supplementary organisational measures, when necessary;

- take measures for appropriate surveillance of the working environment and of workers' health;

- inform workers of potential occupational hazards in the working environment and instruct them in the measures available for the prevention and control of, and protection against, those hazards. All protective and preventive measures and health surveillance shall be free of cost for the worker concerned.

Workers shall co-operate in the fulfilment by their employer of the obligations placed upon them in the field of occupational safety and health, and they shall comply with the safety procedures relating to the prevention and control of, and protection against, occupational hazards in the working environment. Co-operation between management and workers and their representatives within the undertaking shall be an essential element of all measures concerning occupational safety and health.

The general instruments continue to be supplemented by more specific Conventions and Recommendations dealing in greater detail with technical subjects, such as the Asbestos Convention, 1986 (No. 162), and Recommendation (No. 172).

6.1.2 Other ILO guidance

Basic information on health effects of mineral and synthetic fibres and control measures can be found in the ILO's Encyclopaedia of occupational health and safety (third edition, 1983).

Guidance in control of airborne dust in the workplace is provided in a number of ILO codes of practice, in particular in Occupational exposure to airborne substances harmful to health (1980), and Safety in the use of asbestos (1984), as well as in No. 39 of the Occupational Safety and Health Series, Occupational cancer: Prevention and control (second (revised) edition, 1988). The ILO code of practice Safety, health and working conditions in the transfer of technology to developing countries (1988) is also relevant.

Updated information can be provided through the International Occupational Safety and Health Information Centre (CIS) and the International Occupational Safety and Health Hazard Alert System.

6.2 General considerations concerning exposure to mineral and synthetic fibres

The size, shape and physical and chemical properties of each of the fibrous materials considered in this document and the potential risks associated with their manufacture, mining and use vary considerably. The specific nature and extent of appropriate preventive and control measures outlined generally in section 6.3 should be based, therefore, on hazard assessment for each fibre type. Based on this guidance, manufacturers and suppliers should provide additional current advice, appropriate to their products. In all cases the objective should be the reduction of the exposure of people to airborne respirable fibres.

For the purpose of enacting or enforcing occupational health and safety legislation or regulations, hazard assessments should be conducted by the competent government authorities; hazard assessment as a basis for introduction of practical preventive policies and control measures at the workplace is the responsibility of the employer.

The adequacy of the data available upon which to base a hazard assessment varies considerably for the different fibre types considered in this document. For example, the extensive epidemiological and laboratory studies on insulation wools (i.e. rock, slag and glass wools) have been assessed by both IARC and IPCS; whereas the database for refractory, aramid and special purpose glass fibres is much less complete. For respirable fibrous materials for which available data are incomplete, information on fibre size distribution and durability is particularly important in hazard assessment. Durable fibres are those which persist in the lung. Long thin and durable fibres appear to be the most hazardous at the same level of exposure.

When possible, materials containing coarser, less durable fibres, and materials and work practices which minimise the release of respirable fibres should be selected, provided that they are suitable for the purpose of use. In addition, where knowledge is insufficient, preventive and control measures should be implemented on a temporary basis on the understanding that the adequacy of those measures be reviewed in light of new information. It is important that every effort be made to gain such new information. (It is also important that an international agency such as the ILO play a key and active role in the collection, evaluation and dissemination of such information.)

In addition to conducting a hazard assessment, the nature of which will vary depending upon the extent of the available database, other factors which should be taken into consideration in the selection and application of appropriate preventive and control measures include the likely exposure levels and the efficiency of available preventive measures.

On the basis of the principles outlined above, some general conclusions concerning preventive and control measures appropriate for several of the fibrous materials addressed in this report can be drawn. For example, fibrous erionite has been evaluated by IARC as a Group I carcinogen. This evaluation, together with the knowledge that mesotheliomas in humans have resulted from exposure to very low levels of fibrous erionite, and the difficulty in adequately controlling exposure, suggest that the commercial use of fibrous erionite would present a major health hazard.

Available data on disease incidence and mortality in populations exposed to respirable fibre concentrations in the manufacture and use of insulation wools (rock, slag and glasswool) indicate that, with the adoption of appropriate control and preventive measures based on the general recommendations in section 6.3, any risks associated with the production and use of the insulation wools should be minimal.

For continuous filament and many of the synthetic organic fibres, the generation of respirable fibres is unlikely, but precautions are necessary because of the irritant properties of the dust and the potential exposure to toxic chemicals.

Information to serve as a basis for hazard assessment for special purpose glass fibres, refractory fibres and aramid fibres is only sufficient for recommending interim measures based on the guidance in section 6.3. These should be sufficiently stringent to minimise inhalation of respirable fibres and should be reviewed periodically in light of new information. Every attempt should be made to collect additional data as quickly as possible.

Data relevant to hazard evaluation for most of the natural mineral fibres addressed in this report are limited. However, with the exception of fibrous erionite which should not be used commercially, preventive and control measures based on the recommendations in section 6.3 should be adopted in the mining and use of minerals known to release respirable fibres.

For fibrous materials likely to release respirable fibres during mining, production and use, and on which there are no data for making a hazard assessment, stringent preventive and control measures based on the principles outlined in section 6.3 should be adopted.

6.3 Specific considerations concerning exposure to mineral and synthetic fibres

6.3.1 Exposure limits

Appropriate work practices, and engineering and administrative control measures, should aim at controlling the exposure of workers to airborne dust and fibres, and keeping it below the recognised exposure limits or other exposure criteria for the evaluation of the working environment, according to national regulations. In the establishment of these limits or criteria, the type of fibres and their potential health risk shall be taken into account, and the decision taken after consultation with the representatives of the employers and workers concerned, with due regard to advice from competent scientific bodies.

The necessity of establishing exposure limits or other exposure criteria for both total dust and respirable fibre concentrations is based on the following consideration. Some of the mineral and synthetic fibres may contain only a limited proportion of respirable fibres, resulting in low concentrations of respirable fibres in the air. If the exposure limit is established only for respirable fibres, the total dust concentration might be excessively high and cause adverse effects such as the irritation of the respiratory system, eyes and skin. An exposure limit only for total dust may not sufficiently control exposure to respirable fibres.

6.3.2 Labelling

The user of mineral or synthetic fibres or products containing them may not be aware of the composition of the material and potential health hazards. Therefore, producers or suppliers of products containing mineral and synthetic fibres should be made responsible for appropriate labelling of the container or product in accordance with national regulations. Labels should provide basic information such as the trade name of the product, name of the fibrous material, name of the manufacturer and supplier, nature of the specific risk (health hazard), danger symbol, information on safe handling and protective measures. To assist understanding, labels should include simple illustrations (symbols) as well as information written in a language and manner understandable to the workers.

Material safety data sheets should elaborate the above information in more detail.

The information on the labels and in the material safety data sheets should be part of that provided to the worker.

6.3.3 Work practices

Appropriate work practices should contribute to the control of dust and fibres in the air. They should be based on the following principles:

(a) the use and maintenance of machinery, equipment, tools and ventilation systems in accordance with instructions;

(b) wetting where appropriate of products containing fibrous materials before further manipulation;

(c) regular cleaning of machinery and work areas by appropriate methods which do not in themselves generate dust, such as vacuum cleaning or wet cleaning;

(d) proper use of personal protective equipment.

(e) auditing of the work practices and the preventive and control measures.

In view of the continuing development of new types of mineral and synthetic fibres, manufacturers should aim to make products which emit minimum amounts of dust and respirable fibres during their production, manipulation, such as cutting or shaping, installation, removal, and waste disposal. Employers should endeavour to use materials, products and work practices which minimise the release of fibres and dust at work.

The packaging, storage and transport of products should be done in such a manner as to minimise the release of dust and fibres. The finished products should on delivery be packed in such a way that the release of dust from the materials is counteracted. They should also be supplied in a form and shape which enable them to be used with a minimum of adaptation which could release dust and fibres, such as cutting or drilling on site.

6.3.4 Engineering control measures

Engineering control measures should include, as appropriate:

(a) process separation, automation or enclosure;

(b) the bonding of fibres with other materials to prevent generation of dust;

(c) local exhaust ventilation;

(d) general ventilation;

(e) use of wet materials;

(f) use of special tools generating a low level of dust;

(g) separate workplaces for certain processes.

6.3.5 Housekeeping and welfare

Work areas should be cleaned regularly to remove any build-up of dust or fibres. Waste materials should be placed in suitable containers and removed promptly to avoid being trampled and spread about.

Cleaning of the waste should be by vacuum cleaners fitted with appropriate filters; but wet cleaning should be acceptable if vacuum cleaning is not practicable. Blowing with compressed air should not be used as a cleaning method.

Eating, drinking and smoking should not take place in work areas.

6.3.6 Monitoring of the working environment and the exposure of workers

The first step to be taken before measurement of dust concentrations is required should be to check the appropriateness of the work practices and the efficiency of engineering control measures against those recommended. When necessary, appropriate corrective measures should be applied immediately. Consideration should then be given to the monitoring of the working environment.

As regards use, monitoring is important to develop data banks of information on typical dust and fibre levels in as wide a range of uses as possible. It is not practicable to carry out monitoring at all sites for all tasks and the need for monitoring should be determined in relation to the specific nature of the site and tasks, the duration of the tasks and the availability and reliability of data on assessment or measurement, carried out elsewhere in similar types of work.

In manufacture, sites should be regularly monitored. If there are no changes in the manufacturing process, two-year intervals may suffice. Monitoring frequency should increase if there are changes in the manufacturing process, including change in binders and change in production rate, or changes in the engineering control measures.

Both fixed site (area or static) and personal monitoring should be carried out. Static monitoring, particularly in treatment plants, is important to evaluate the efficiency of engineering control measures. Personal monitoring is important to provide estimates of the average exposure which employees experience in different tasks. Both total airborne dust and fibre count should be monitored.

Besides fibrous materials, other air contaminants may also need to be monitored, such as quartz or erionite in natural fibrous minerals, or various chemical substances in the production and use of MMMF and synthetic organic fibres.

The determination of dust and airborne respirable fibre concentrations should be made in accordance with national regulations, by persons trained and experienced in sampling techniques and analytical procedures.

The results of monitoring should be made available to employees, their representatives in the enterprise, and to occupational health services responsible for the surveillance of the health of the workers. The records of the results should be retained by employers for the period corresponding to the latency time of the associated disease. In the case of cancer, a period of at least 30 years seems to be appropriate.

6.3.7 Personal protective equipment

If it is reasonable to believe that established exposure limits for dust or respirable fibres are being exceeded, measures should be taken to lower the concentration. If such measures are impracticable or insufficient, appropriate respiratory protective equipment should be provided and worn until the task is completed, or until monitoring has established levels of dust and respirable fibres below the national standard.

The respiratory protection used should conform with the appropriate standards to protect against the particular levels of dust or respirable fibres. Respirators should be tested for adequate fit. They should be stored and maintained in clean working order.

Eye protection, in the form of appropriate safety glasses, goggles, or face shields, should be worn during overhead work and where dust levels are likely to be high.

Skin irritation should be minimised by the wearing of gloves, loose-fitting long-sleeved shirts with a cloth tucked inside the collar, and long trousers.

Adequate washing and changing facilities should be provided. Work clothing should be provided for the workers. It should be regularly washed separately from other laundry to avoid cross-contamination and possible subsequent skin irritation of other workers.

6.3.8 Instruction, training, and information

People exposed to mineral and synthetic fibres should be provided with all available information on the potential health effects of these materials. The information should be sufficiently detailed to ensure an understanding of these effects, and the precautions necessary to avoid them.

Managers, supervisors and employees should receive instruction and training to enable them all to assume their responsibilities and to perform their tasks safely. This should include: correct work practices; engineering controls, including ventilation equipment; and the use and maintenance of personal protective clothing and equipment. The extent of instruction and training should be appropriate to the duties of the individuals within the organisation, and be sufficiently detailed to ensure that the individual understands not only the procedural and safety requirements, but also the reasons for these requirements.

6.3.9 Health surveillance

Regular health surveillance should be offered to all those who are exposed to dusts in production or use. The health surveillance should commence at the time of employment and then be carried out at intervals established by occupational health services, taking into account the type of the health hazard, level of exposure and health status of the worker.

The examination should include personal and occupational history, smoking history and clinical examination, and may be complemented by other examinations and tests, as appropriate and in accordance with national regulations. The purpose of the examination is to evaluate the health of the worker in relation to exposure to airborne fibres and other hazardous agents in the workplace, and the worker's ability to use personal protective equipment.

The results of the health surveillance should be communicated to the worker. These results should remain confidential to each person, but the overall results at each site should be analysed for significant trends. The medical records should be kept for the period corresponding to the latency time of the disease associated with the exposure to fibrous dust. In the case of cancer, a period of at least 30 years seems to be appropriate.

Whenever possible, the results of health surveillance should be linked with the results of monitoring the exposure.

7. LAW AND PRACTICE IN SELECTED COUNTRIES

This chapter is based on replies to a request for
information on non-asbestos natural and man-made fibrous
materials, sent by the ILO to all national designated bodies of
the International Hazard Alert System in 1986 and updated in
1988. The replies summarised in this report were received from
the following countries: Australia, Belgium, Bolivia, Botswana,
Bulgaria, Cameroon, Canada, Chile, Colombia, Côte d'Ivoire,
Cyprus, Czechoslovakia, Denmark, Dominican Republic, Ecuador,
Egypt, Federal Republic of Germany, Finland, German Democratic
Republic, Ghana, Guinea-Bissau, Japan, Kuwait, Madagascar,
Malaysia, Malawi, Malta, Mauritius, Netherlands, New Zealand,
Nigeria, Norway, Pakistan, Philippines, Poland, Qatar, Rwanda,
Seychelles, Singapore, Spain, Sri Lanka, Sweden, United Republic
of Tanzania, Trinidad and Tobago, Tunisia, Turkey, United
Kingdom, United States, USSR and Uruguay. The ILO wishes to
thank all these countries for their co-operation.

7.1 Production and use of man-made mineral fibres

Man-made mineral fibres are used in all countries which
responded to the questionnaire, whereas production is restricted
to some of them.

Glasswool (and filament) and rockwool (including slagwool,
mostly not distinguished in the replies) manufacturing was
reported by a number of countries: Australia, Bulgaria (only
glasswool), Chile, Czechoslovakia, Denmark, Finland, Japan,
Malaysia (rockwool), Netherlands, New Zealand, Nigeria
(glasswool), Norway, Poland, Singapore (glasswool), Spain,
Sweden, United States, USSR and Uruguay (glasswool).

Other types of synthetic fibres are reportedly produced less
frequently: carbon fibres in Japan, Spain, Sweden and United
States; ceramic fibres in Japan, Spain, United States and
Uruguay; and steel fibres in Japan and Netherlands.

Glass and rock fibres have the most uses: glasswool for
thermal insulation (construction industry, insulation of pipes,
etc.); glassfibre textile for the manufacture of reinforced
plastic products (parts of cars, boats, containers, furniture,
etc.); rockwool for thermal insulation, but also for sound-
absorbing ceilings and walls (as hardboard) or mixed with cement
or adhesives for spraying on to inner and outer walls and for
brake linings; ceramic fibres for special heat insulation in the

iron and steel industry; carbon fibres for sports equipment and space development material; and many other uses.

Amounts of fibrous materials annually used (in thousands of tons) as communicated by the countries in 1986 are summarised in the following table.

Table 4.   Amounts of materials annually used
           in selected countries, 1986
           (in thousands of tons)

Country	Rockwool	Glasswool	Glass filament	Total MMMF
Australia	9	18	–	–
Finland	71	9	–	–
Japan	245	136	253	–
Malaysia	0.95	–	0.6	–
New Zealand	2.8	4.5	2	–
Nigeria	–	5 to 6	–	–
Poland	–	–	–	150
Singapore	several	several	–	–
Spain	6 (production)	–	–	–
United States	–	–	8.5 (production)	–

Although the data are incomplete, they indicate the extent of the use. Besides the materials given in the table, Finland reports the use of 2,000 tons of wollastonite and New Zealand of 10 tons of Kevlar[R] aramid and 1 ton of carbon fibres.

The amount of man-made mineral fibres used in Sweden is estimated to be about $5 \times 10^6 m^3$ per year.

According to the information provided by the Industrieverband Chemiefaser E.V. (Federal Republic of Germany), the world production of glassfibres in 1987 reached 1.6 million tons, 3,000 tons of carbon fibres and 2.5 million tons of acrylic fibres. In 1988, 3.7 million tons of polyamide, 8.1 million tons polyester and 30,000 tons aramid fibres were produced.

7.2 Regulations

7.2.1 General and specific regulations

Almost all respondents replied that the work involving exposure to airborne fibrous materials is covered by general regulations on occupational health and safety. Their aim is to provide for the prevention of health impairment due to occupational exposure to harmful substances. These regulations usually require that the occupiers of undertakings take all necessary steps to ensure that workers are protected against inhalation of any dust likely to be injurious by the adoption of appropriate work practices, by engineering control measures (in particular, ventilation) and by the use of personal protective clothing and equipment (e.g. overalls and respirators), inter alia.

The only specific regulations reported are the Swedish Ordinance (AFS 1982:4) concerning Synthetic Inorganic Fibres, issued by the National Swedish Board of Occupational Safety and Health on 18 March 1982 and the United Kingdom Guidance Note EH 46 from the Health and Safety Executive of 1986: Exposure to mineral wool. The former applies to materials containing more than 5 per cent by weight of such fibres. Both regulations give general guidance on health risks, work practices, control measures and monitoring. In Norway, the use of attapulgite and sepiolite in the oil industry has been prohibited and regulations for man-made mineral fibres are in preparation.

7.2.2 Labelling

The Swedish regulations provide for labelling of packages containing man-made mineral fibres; labelling is not necessary for insulation wool products if they are easily identifiable. No specific requirements were reported by other countries and labelling is provided for by general regulations concerning labelling of materials considered dangerous.

7.2.3 Exposure limits

Some countries have established specific exposure limits, in particular for MMMF, whereas others refer to exposure limits for nuisance dust which are frequently 10 mg total dust/m^3 or 5 mg respirable dust/m^3.

The following countries reported specific exposure limits:

Bulgaria

- MMMF, fibre diameter above 3 μm, total dust   3 mg/m^3

- MMMF, fibre diameter below 3 μm, total dust   2 mg/m^3

respirable dust   0.2 mg/m^3

fibre concentration   3 f/ml

Czechoslovakia

- MMMF, total dust (as mineral dust without

fibrogenous properties)   8 mg/m^3

- proposing to lower it to   4 mg/m^3

and establish an exposure limit for

respirable fibres   0.2 f/ml

Both limits could be accepted alternatively.

Denmark

- MMMF (rock, slag and glasswool):

  stationary workplaces   2 f/ml

non-stationary workplaces, total dust   5 mg/m^3

Federal Republic of Germany

- general dust   6 mg/m^3

The exposure limit is currently under revision.

Finland

- wollastonite, recommended   5 mg/m^3

German Democratic Republic

- mineral fibrous dust without asbestos:

  TWA   2 mg/m^3

A research project, scheduled to be completed in 1990 involves a study of the separation characteristics of MMMF in the respiratory tract, the identification of the practical requirements of measuring and analysing methods, and the establishment of a new exposure limit for MMMF.

Japan

An "administrative level" E is prescribed for mineral dusts:

$$E = \frac{2.9}{0.22\ Q + 1}\ \text{mg/m}^3, \text{ where } Q = \text{free silica content (%)}$$

New Zealand

- MMMF, total dust   5 mg/m³

- MMMF, fibre diameter less than 3 µm   less than 1 f/ml

Although these levels apply simultaneously, whichever is the more restrictive criterion would depend on the characteristics of the particular fibre involved.

Poland

- MMMF, total dust   4 mg/m³

- MMMF, fibre length exceeding 5 µm   2 f/ml

Sweden

New Ordinance AFS 1987:12 came into force on 1 July 1988. The LLV (level limit value) for synthetic inorganic fibres (=MMMF) has been lowered to 1 f/ml. The LLV is a limit value for exposure during a full working day.

United Kingdom

- MMMF, total dust, control limit (maximum
      exposure limit from October 1989)   5 mg/m³

- MMMF, fibre count, maximum exposure limit
      under examination   2 f/ml

United States

OSHA permissible exposure limit (PEL) is under revision

NIOSH recommended exposure limit (REL), TWA for
      fibrous glass, rockwool and graphite fibres

- total dust   5 mg/m³

- fibre diameter less than or equal to
  3.5 µm, length greater or equal to
  10 µm, fibre concentration   3 f/ml

USSR

Total dust:

- MMMF: silicates, aluminosilicates with
          vitreous structure (glassfibres,
          glasswool, mineral wool, slagwool
          mullite based fibres with CR^{3+}
          content of up to 5% by weight)   2 mg/m^3

- Carbon fibrous material on the basis of
  hydrate cellulose or PAN:

          short-term limit (30 min)   4 mg/m^3
          TWA   2 mg/m^3

7.2.4 Monitoring of exposure to dust at the workplace

No specific regulations have in general been issued and the matter is usually covered by a general occupational health and safety regulation concerning work involving exposure to airborne dust (e.g. in Japan measurement at the workplace is required at least every six months).

In Denmark the principle of an exposure zone screening limit value is applied which consists of the gravimetric measurement of total dust concentration. Only samples which exceed the above limit are evaluated for respirable fibre concentration.

7.2.5 Health examination of workers

No specific regulations have been reported and the matter is generally covered by provisions concerning medical examination of workers. Japan refers to its regulations concerning medical examinations in case of risk of pneumoconioses. In Finland periodical check-ups are usually carried out every three to five years in plants producing or using fibrous materials; in Poland at two- to three-year intervals.

7.3 Additional information

A few data exist on the actual concentrations of airborne dust in the workplace. In Australia the average concentrations are about 2 mg/m^3 total dust, or 0.5 mg/m^3 respirable fraction. In Czechoslovakia 0.2 to 4.5 mg total dust/m^3 are currently found in glassfibre production, which corresponds to 0.02 to 0.4 fibre/ml. In Denmark 0.05 to 3 f/ml were found at workplaces where mineral wool was used. In Finland the current concentrations of glasswool are found to be 0.1 to 2.5 mg/m^3, i.e. less than 0.1 fibre/ml; however, in blasting bulk wool for insulation, 1 fibre/ml may occur. In New Zealand 0.45 f/ml were found in the use of rockwool. In Poland total dust concentrations in the range of 9.41 to 15.58 mg/m^3 and respirable dust 0.05 to 1.41 f/ml were found in the manufacturing of MMMF.

Special attention is paid to the prevention of exposure to superfine fibres (diameter less than 0.3 μm, such as those found in glasswool used for earplugs for protection against noise) (Sweden, United Kingdom).

The number of workers exposed may be quite high. In the United States almost 38,000 workers are exposed to rockwool. In Poland some 2,000 workers are employed in manufacturing MMMF. A very important observation has been made by the Netherlands: namely, that man-made mineral fibres are frequently used in small-scale industry, such as the manufacturing of glass-reinforced plastics, shipbuilding, engineering, construction industry, production of refrigerators, etc.

ANNEX 1

RESOLUTION CONCERNING THE DEVELOPMENT OF PREVENTIVE
AND PROTECTIVE MEASURES RELATED TO THE HEALTH RISKS
ASSOCIATED WITH OCCUPATIONAL EXPOSURE TO FIBRES,
WHETHER NATURAL OR ARTIFICIAL (ADOPTED BY THE
INTERNATIONAL LABOUR CONFERENCE AT ITS
72ND SESSION, 1986)

The General Conference of the International Labour Organisation,

Recalling the resolution concerning the improvement of working conditions and environment and the conclusions concerning future action in the field of working conditions and environment adopted at the 70th Session of the International Labour Conference in 1984,

Noting with concern that the use of dangerous substances and the potential risks involved in the production, stocking and distribution of these substances may entail an increase in the occupational hazards faced by large numbers of workers,

Noting the need to evaluate the health risks associated with occupational exposure to dangerous substances and to prevent and control exposure that places workers at risk,

Stressing the corresponding importance of training and further training for all those who in the course of their work are or will be exposed to the hazards inherent in the use of dangerous substances,

Recognising that the full and active participation of the workers and of their organisations is essential to the protection of health and prevention of accidents and to the improvement of working conditions and environment,

Welcoming the increased efforts of the International Labour Office to strengthen and improve its supervision and its activities aimed at eliminating the major risks from the use of dangerous substances,

Bearing in mind the discussion during the 71st and 72nd Sessions of the International Labour Conference (1985 and 1986) on safety in the use of asbestos,

Expressing its concern at the potential risks that the use of fibres, whether natural or artificial, may entail;

1. Invites the Governing Body of the International Labour Office to request the Director-General —

(a) to expedite the health risk assessment of inorganic fibres, whether natural or artificial, other than asbestos, currently under way by the United Nations Environmental Programme/International Labour Office/World Health Organization (International Programme on Chemical Safety), and to also undertake as soon as possible, the assessment of organic fibres by the Programme;

(b) to set up, within the limits of the approved ILO resources, a tripartite group of experts, representing all the regions, to study the question of preventive and protective measures related to the occupational health risks due to exposure to fibres, whether natural or artificial, other than asbestos;

(c) to consider the need to draft relevant instruments;

(d) to strengthen the International Labour Office's technical co-operation and standard-setting activities with the objective to implement the preventive and protective measures related to the occupational health risks associated with exposure to fibres, whether natural or artificial, and to strengthen accordingly the Office's co-operation with other competent United Nations agencies, particularly the World Health Organisation and the United Nations Environment Programme;

(e) to emphasise, in the technical assistance and advisory services provided by the International Labour Office in the fields of training, labour inspection and workers' education, the protential health risks arising from occupational exposure to all fibres, whether natural or artificial, and the necessary preventive and protective measures to be taken.

2. Invites the Governing Body of the International Labour Office to call on all member States, on the basis of information already available, to promulgate and implement appropriate laws and guide-lines for establishing safety and health standards and conditions in the mining, manufacture, handling and use of certain types of fibres, whether natural or artificial, and to ensure the active participation of the workers' and employers' organisations in the drafting enforcement of these provisions.

3. Invites the Governing Body of the International Labour Office to call on all member States exporting fibres, whether natural or artificial, to assume an active role in bilateral as well as multilateral technical co-operation.

ANNEX 2

REPORT OF THE
MEETING OF EXPERTS ON SAFETY IN THE USE OF
MINERAL AND SYNTHETIC FIBRES

(Geneva, 17-25 April 1989)

---

1.   At its 239th Session (February-March 1988), the Governing Body decided to convene a meeting of Experts on Safety in the Use of Mineral and Synthetic Fibres (Except Asbestos). The meeting was held in Geneva from 17 to 25 April 1989.

Agenda of the meeting

2.   The agenda of the meeting based on the Governing Body decision consisted of the following items indicated in the resolution of the 72nd Session of the International Labour Conference concerning the development of preventive and protective measures related to the health risks associated with the occupational exposure to fibres, whether natural or artificial:

- to study the question of preventive and protective measures related to the occupational health risks due to exposure to fibres, whether natural or artificial, other than asbestos;

- to consider the need to draft relevant instruments;

- to examine measures to strengthen the ILO's technical co-operation with the objective of implementing the preventive and protective measures related to occupational health risks associated with exposure to the fibres under consideration;

- to examine measures for ILO support for training, labour inspection and workers' education in this field.

Participants

3.   Fifteen experts were invited to the meeting, five of them after consultation with Governments, five after consultation

with the Employers' group and five after consultation with the Workers' group of the Governing Body.

4.   Several   observers   also   attended   the   meeting, representing   the   World   Health   Organization   (WHO),   the International Commission on Occupational Health (ICOH), the International Confederation of Free Trade Unions (ICFTU), the International Organisation of Employers (IOE), the International Social Security Association (ISSA), the World Confederation of Labour (WCL), the World Federation of Trade Unions (WFTU), the Asbestos International Association (AIA), the European Insulation Manufacturers' Association (EURIMA), the International Federation of Building and Woodworkers (IFBWW), the International Federation of Chemical, Energy and General Workers' Union (IFCEGWU), the International Textile, Garment and Leather Workers' Federation (ITGLWF), the Thermal Insulation Manufacturers' Association (TIMA), the Joint European Medical Research Board (JEMRB) and the Trade Unions International of Workers of the Building, Wood and Building Materials Industries.

5.   The list of participants is annexed to the report.

Opening address

6.   The meeting was opened by Mr. V. Morozov, Assistant Director-General of the ILO. He welcomed the participants to the meeting and expressed his pleasure in noting the presence of representatives   of   other   international   organisations   and observers   from   employers'   and   workers'   organisations.   He expressed his particular satisfaction with the representation of the World Health Organization which had significantly contributed to the evaluation of the health effects of the natural and man-made mineral fibres. Of particular importance was the work of the International Agency for Research on Cancer and the International Programme on Chemical Safety, a joint activity of the ILO, the WHO and the United Nations Environment Programme.

7.   Mr. Morozov pointed out that the meeting was an event in the continuum of activities of the ILO concerning the protection of workers against disease and injury arising out of their employment. He recalled that among the many ILO activities in the field of occupational health, the prevention and control of occupational health hazards due to the exposure of workers to airborne dust had always held an important position. He referred to the international pneumoconioses conferences convened by the ILO and the ILO International Classification of Radiographs of Pneumoconioses. The ILO had given assistance to member States for the assessment and control of exposure to dust in industry and mining through a number of seminars, meetings of relevant industrial committees, publications, codes of practice and projects of technical co-operation.

8.   He drew attention to the ILO's activities concerning safety in the use of asbestos. They included the publication of the code of practice, _Safety in the use of asbestos_, in 1984 and the adoption of the Asbestos Convention (No. 162) and Recommendation (No. 172) in 1986. The International Labour Conference, when adopting the Asbestos Convention and Recommendation, expressed its concern about the health risks associated with occupational exposure to fibres, whether natural or artificial, and adopted a resolution on the development of preventive and protective measures. This meeting had been convened in response to the resolution. The participants' advice was sought with a view to providing sufficient protection for the workers exposed to mineral and synthetic fibres and securing the appropriate use of potentially beneficial materials. He reminded the participants that they were attending the meeting in their personal capacity as experts, and wished for constructive deliberations.

Election of Chairman

9.   Mr. K.C. Gupta was unanimously elected as Chairman and Reporter of the meeting.

Presentation of the working document

10.   The meeting had before it a working paper on safety in the use of mineral and synthetic fibres. The working paper was presented by Dr. K. Kogi, representative of the Director-General. The working paper dealt with the occupational exposure and health effects of mineral and synthetic fibres and the preventive and control measures including law and practice in selected countries. The chapters on man-made mineral fibres and natural mineral fibres were based on the evaluation of these materials by the WHO, in particular through the ILO/WHO/UNEP International Programme on Chemical Safety (IPCS), and the International Agency for Research on Cancer (IARC), whereas the chapter on synthetic fibres could not be backed by similar analyses.

11.   He invited the experts to discuss the working paper based on their experience. The publication by the Office of the revised working paper would benefit the users of mineral and synthetic fibres in implementing practical preventive and control measures. The views of the experts would make a valuable contribution towards the joint effort of governments, industry and workers to control such hazards at places of work.

Discussion of the working paper

General discussion

12.   In the general discussion, it was agreed to retain the definition of a respirable fibre as a particle with a diameter of less than 3 µm and of which the length was at least three times the diameter, in conformity with that used for a respirable asbestos fibre by the ILO code of practice, Safety in the use of asbestos, and other documents.   It was argued that any change in the definition at this time would lead to confusion.   However, in view of new knowledge of the health effects of fibres of various sizes, it was felt that there was a need for its revision in the near future.

13.   It was a general consensus that the working paper should be based on the evaluation of health effects made by the WHO International Agency for Research on Cancer (IARC) and the International Programme on Chemical Safety (IPCS) when this was available.

14.   A question was raised about the appropriateness of the title of the working paper referring to safety in the use of fibres, with an argument that a safe working environment without any risks was unrealistic.   It was explained that safety in this context was considered to be achievable and did not mean a no-risk condition in absolute terms.   Some experts referred to the title of the ILO Convention concerning safety in the use of asbestos, where safety was accepted as an objective.   The experts agreed that it would not be beneficial to users of the document to have a title different from that of related asbestos documents.   The experts agreed to keep the proposed title.

15.   A question was also raised on which base the fibres dealt with in the working paper had been chosen.   Reference was made to the decision of the Governing Body to convene this meeting to deal with mineral and synthetic fibres and to the definition of man-made fibres given in the ILO's Encyclopaedia of occupational health and safety (third edition, 1983).   Man-made fibres were divided into synthetic fibres, which included organic synthetic fibres derived from monomeric chemicals and man-made mineral fibres, and artificial fibres of natural vegetable or animal origin.   In conformity with the terms of reference of the meeting, only the synthetic fibres were discussed.   As regards man-made mineral fibres, the experts agreed to apply the nomenclature used in the IPCS document, Man-made mineral fibres, Environmental health criteria 77, published by the WHO in 1988. It was mentioned that the term fibres used in this meeting covered both respirable and non-respirable fibres, and that health effects and control measures would refer primarily to respirable fibres.

16. The experts discussed whether possible effects due to the chemicals associated with the production and use of the fibrous materials should be taken into consideration. It was agreed that, where appropriate, chemical risks should be considered.

Man-made mineral fibres

17. The experts followed the IPCS classification of man-made mineral fibres as insulation wool (including glasswool, rockwool and slagwool), refractory fibres (including ceramic fibres), continuous filament, and special purpose fibres. They noted that the possibility for harmful effects on the health of workers exposed to these fibres was supported by results of animal experiments and some epidemiological evidence. It was noted, on the other hand, that changes over time in the manufacturing process had enabled significant improvements in the final products with a subsequent reduction in airborne respirable fibres.

18. The results of recent research into the health effects of man-made mineral fibres were discussed extensively. Some experts noted that, in addition to irritant dermatitis and eye irritation, allergic reactions to chemical agents used in production occasionally occurred. Available data summarised by the IPCS showed that there was no clear evidence that populations occupationally exposed to these fibres had suffered from non-malignant respiratory disease (including fibrosis of the lungs). The epidemiological data on cancer mortality and incidence, also summarised by the IPCS, showed an excess of mortality due to lung cancer among rockwool/slagwool production workers employed in an early production phase, but not in production of glasswool and continuous filaments. There had not been any evidence that mesotheliomas were associated with occupational exposures to insulation wools or continuous filament. No epidemiological data were available on lung cancer or mesothelioma incidence in refractory fibre workers. The IARC evaluation indicated that glasswool, rockwool, slagwool and refractory (ceramic) fibres were possibly carcinogenic to humans (Group 2B), and that continuous filaments were not classifiable as to their carcinogenicity to humans due to inadequate information.

19. The experts noted the IPCS evaluation that cancer risk could be increased for some workers in the ceramic fibre and small diameter (less than 1 µm) glasswool fibre manufacturing sectors if appropriate engineering control measures were lacking, and for workers engaged in blowing or spraying of insulation wool in confined spaces if working without protective measures. They also noted that the possible risk of lung cancer among the

general public was very low and should not be a cause for concern under the current low levels of exposure.

Natural mineral fibres
(other than asbestos)

20.   The experts noted that a wide range of naturally occurring minerals existed in a fibrous form, and that they contained fibres of respirable sizes.   The list of such minerals was extensive, but the experts agreed that erionite, attapulgite and wollastonite were the subject of discussion because of their potential for occupational exposure and the availability of an extensive review by the IPCS and IARC.   It was also noted that these minerals did not always occur in a fibrous form.

21.   It was pointed out that there were some other minerals which contained fibrous particles and were widely used, such as gypsum, but that there had been few studies concerning their health effects.   In fact, very few of the fibrous minerals had been tested in experimental systems.   The experts also considered that the limited evidence available for those minerals indicated that the potential health effects would differ widely.   It was felt that employers should therefore obtain information on the possible occupational exposures to fibrous particles in these materials.

22.   According to the IARC evaluation, erionite was seen to be more potent than crocidolite in causing mesothelioma following low environmental exposures.   The results of small prevalence studies suggested that attapulgite and wollastonite could cause pneumoconiotic changes (lung fibrosis) in humans.   Animal experiments provided limited evidence for carcinogenicity of attapulgite and wollastonite.

23.   The experts noted that airborne dust samples from certain mining or milling operations of erionite or attapulgite showed the presence of respirable dust to a limited extent.   The exposures to wollastonite were reported to be associated with higher workplace concentrations.   Some experts pointed out that community exposures of erionite could also be associated with potential risk.

Synthetic organic fibres

24.   Among the variety of synthetic organic fibres made from polymers, the experts agreed to select three materials, aramid fibres, carbon/graphite fibres, and polyolefin fibres because of their potential for generating airborne respirable fibres and because of the availability of information on them.   The experts expressed their reservation on the validity of the assessment of

the health effects of these materials, as no evaluation was available by the IPCS or IARC.

25. The experts agreed that there was evidence that at high concentrations, certain para-aramid fibres could cause fibrosis and lung tumours in animal inhalation studies. The experts pointed out that in the case of para-aramid fibres, the user exposures of most concern were those where product was used in the pulp form to make friction materials or the staple form to spin yarn. The other current uses of para-aramid fibres were not associated with the potential for release of respirable fibres.

26. While carbon/graphite fibres might break during processing to generate respirable dust particles, results of airborne respirable fibre monitoring were not available. Polyolefins were mostly large diameter fibres, and the potential for airborne respirable fibres was considered to be less of a problem. There was no information on the health effects of polyolefins. There were no available data on non-occupational exposures to synthetic organic fibres nor on their possible effects on health.

Monitoring of the working
environment

27. The experts agreed that monitoring of the working environment included: surveillance and auditing of the efficiency of control and preventive measures, such as (1) engineering controls, (2) selection of materials and equipment, (3) work practices and (4) ventilation; and measurements of dust and fibre concentrations and surveillance of health hazards arising from exposure to mineral and synthetic fibres.

28. The experts agreed that the measurement of airborne concentrations of respirable fibres in the working environment according to established methods was vital for effective control measures. They noted that training and quality control in the use of measurement techniques was critical to avoid inaccurate results. It was agreed to describe general methods available for the measurement of the concentrations of the total airborne dusts and respirable fibres in the working environment.

29. With respect to gravimetric determination of total airborne dusts, the principles of a gravimetric method of measuring airborne dust containing asbestos fibres, as referred to in the ILO code of practice, Safety in the use of asbestos, could be applied to any type of mineral and synthetic fibres.

30. For determination of airborne respirable fibre concentrations, the three methods provided by the ILO code of practice, the WHO Regional Office for Europe and the United

States National Institute of Occupational Safety and Health were mentioned. They were based on the widely used membrane filter method. The experts noted that differences in the methods could influence the results of the evaluation of the dust concentrations. Several methods for assessing airborne concentrations of synthetic organic fibres, including those permitting separation of the respirable fraction, were also mentioned.

Preventive and control methods

31. The experts noted that the size, shape and physical and chemical properties of each of the fibrous materials considered, and the potential risks associated with their manufacture, mining and use, varied considerably. The specific nature and extent of appropriate preventive and control measures should be based, therefore, on hazard assessment for each fibre type. Based on this guidance, manufacturers and suppliers should provide additional current advice, appropriate to their products. In all cases the objective should be the reduction of the exposure of people to airborne respirable fibres.

32. The experts agreed that the general principles in the ILO Conventions and Recommendations and codes of practice for the protection of the health of workers against harmful agents at work should be applied also to work with mineral and synthetic fibres. Particular emphasis was placed on well co-ordinated implementation of national level activities and enterprise obligations set out in the most general instruments in this field. General measures prescribed by national law or regulations for the prevention and control of occupational hazards, including design, construction and layout of undertakings, and work processes were considered essential also in the use of fibrous materials. The need for referring, as appropriate, to the principles outlined in specific instruments was also stressed.

33. At the enterprise level, the employers' responsibility for ensuring that the workplaces, machinery, equipment and processes under their control were safe and without risk to workers' health was emphasised. This should include measures for appropriate surveillance of the working environment and of workers' health as well as education and training. Co-operation of workers in the fulfilment by their employer of these obligations was essential. The experts felt that national authorities should help small enterprises in taking the necessary preventive and control measures.

34. The experts further elaborated on specific considerations concerning exposure to fibrous materials. It was pointed out that appropriate work practice and engineering and

administrative control measures should aim at controlling the exposure of workers to airborne dust and fibres, and keep them below the recognised exposure limits or other exposure criteria for the evaluation of the working environment according to national regulations. Some mineral and synthetic fibres might contain only a limited proportion of respirable fibres, resulting in low concentrations of respirable fibres in the air. Should the exposure limit be established only for respirable fibres, the total dust concentration might be excessively high causing adverse effects such as the irritation of the respiratory system, eyes and skin. Thus the experts agreed that both the total dust and the level of respirable fibres should be controlled and kept below established exposure limits or other exposure criteria for the evaluation of the working environment.

35. The experts agreed that producers and suppliers of fibrous materials should inform users of hazards and their prevention whereas the responsibility of informing the working staff rested with the employers. The experts considered that it was important to raise the awareness of all the users with due consideration of the hazards inherent in various fibrous materials. The need for risk evaluation of all individual fibrous materials was stressed.

36. The experts emphasised that, when possible, materials containing coarser, less durable fibres and methods which were to minimise the release of respirable fibres should be selected, provided they were suitable for the purpose of use. The experts agreed that stringent preventive and control measures should be adopted for the mining, production and use of fibrous materials likely to release respirable fibres on which there was little information for making a hazard assessment.

37. The experts emphasised that products likely to release respirable fibres should be appropriately labelled and supplied with material safety data sheets as established by the competent authority. Labels should provide basic information on health hazards and their prevention, and be designed so as to make the information understandable to individual workers using or handling these products and in accordance with national requirements.

38. Particular attention was drawn to appropriate work practices, control measures, and housekeeping for controlling dust and fibres in the air. The experts felt that the use of personal protective equipment should be recommended only where appropriate technical methods according to good industrial practice were not sufficient. Among control measures, process separation or enclosure, choice of processes generating a minimum amount of dust and respirable fibres, the bonding of fibres with other materials to prevent generation of dust and local exhaust ventilation at source should be given a higher priority.

Adequate washing and changing facilities as well as suitable work clothing which should be washed separately to avoid cross-contamination should be provided.

39. Further, the first step to be taken before measurement of dust concentrations should be to check the appropriateness of the work practices and efficiency of engineering control measures. It was considered generally not practicable to carry out monitoring of exposure at all sites for all tasks and therefore the need for monitoring should be determined in relation to the specific nature of the site and tasks, the duration of the tasks, and the availability and reliability of existing data obtained elsewhere in the type of industry concerned.

40. The experts emphasised the need to evaluate personal exposure data together with medical records. Some experts informed the meeting that in some countries projects were ongoing to install systems of records of medical information including occupational exposures to harmful substances in the working environment. Provision was made for the maintenance of such records to assure their availability, in terms which will protect individual privacy and confidentiality with personal identification by competent medical personnel only, for epidemiological and other research. The experts agreed that while the confidentiality of such records was essential, it was important to be able to evaluate the health of the worker in relation to exposure to airborne fibres and other hazardous agents in the workplace.

Law and practice in selected countries

41. The experts noted that a number of countries had provided necessary information about law and practice concerning the topic of the meeting by obtaining updated information. Necessary additions and corrections were made. It was also noted that some countries were in the process of changing relevant regulations.

Promotion of preventive and protective measures in work with synthetic and mineral fibres (other than asbestos)

42. The experts noted the need to urge all concerned to provide information as a basis for hazard evaluation for new materials likely to release airborne fibres during mining, production and use before these materials were marketed and used. Provision of additional information on existing materials for which data to serve as a basis for hazard assessment were

inadequate should also be encouraged. Such new information could be relayed to the ILO through the International Occupational Safety and Health Hazard Alert System.

43. The experts agreed to request the IPCS to undertake the assessment of synthetic organic fibres, as already mentioned in the resolution of the 72nd Session of the International Labour Conference. The ILO should work closely with the WHO and other international organisations in maintaining a data bank which would help classify materials according to the risks they represented. The need for developing a standard protocol for laboratory testing of potential toxicological effects of fibres was stressed, and it was suggested that the IPCS develop such a standard protocol.

44. Considerable discussion took place on the question of preparing an ILO code of practice for certain fibres which could be easily defined and for which sufficient data were available, such as insulation wools. Some experts noted that the risks of these fibres, which were not the most hazardous, had often been exaggerated, but that they involved large numbers of persons all over the world. It was noted that the industry producing such fibres had been aware of the health aspects of its products and had worked closely with scientists for developing guide-lines for safety in their use. The experts felt that it was precisely because a large amount of work on safety had been done by the industry that a code of practice, specifically on insulation wools, was suggested.

45. The experts unanimously agreed to recommend the preparation of a code of practice on safety in the use of insulation wools. It was suggested that a code of practice could benefit both the industry and workers and would be particularly useful for developing countries. In view of the amount of information available, it was possible to prepare such a code quickly.

46. The experts agreed that pending the preparation of such a code, information sharing on potential hazards and control measures in the use of various fibres should continue. The experts called attention to the rapid rate of growth of the fibre industries and noted that pre-testing of these materials was important and that the IPCS and other relevant bodies should pursue health risk studies including those of end users. The importance of the review of definition of fibres and of their classification was stressed.

Possibility of international instruments

47. The meeting considered that the adoption of a new international instrument or instruments concerning the safety in the use of mineral and synthetic fibres was premature. It was the general consensus that it would be useful to concentrate initially on drafting a code of practice as referred to earlier and, in the interim, on sharing information and experience on various fibres.

Strengthening of technical co-operation

48. The meeting discussed different ways of strengthening the ILO's technical co-operation activities particularly in developing countries with the objective of implementing the preventive and protective measures in work with synthetic and mineral fibres. Development of various activities using both the regular budget technical co-operation funds and the extra-budgetary resources was discussed. In view of the characteristics of the problems associated with the use of these fibres, particular attention was drawn to the need of organising workshops, seminars and training courses. Provision of practical advice and guidance on preventive measures and monitoring of the working environment was essential.

49. It was pointed out that there was anxiety among the workers concerned due to the lack of information. Sharing of information was thus vital. Development and dissemination of appropriate information materials through technical co-operation was urgent.

50. The experts agreed on the need for quality control in the monitoring of the working environment by introducing appropriate systems or centres for such work. This should include guidance on monitoring equipment and procedures.

51. The experts noted that different levels of standards in different countries made transfer of technology from one country to another, including transfer of fibre-related technology, an acute problem. The countries which transferred technology on these fibres to developing countries should also ensure the transfer of know-how about preventive and protective measures. Together with the equipment and technology transferred to the recipient country, there should be consistent efforts at providing technical expertise and guidance on these measures. The meeting was informed that initiatives should come from the recipient countries. The ILO's assistance in identifying priority actions and formulating proposals for technical co-operation, keeping in mind the particular expertise required to deal with fibrous materials, was emphasised.

ILO support in education and training

52. The experts emphasised the need for organising education and training in safety in the use of mineral and synthetic fibres at various levels. The target groups should include management, supervisory staff, workers as well as labour inspectors and occupational safety and health personnel. The experts agreed that such training should be part of comprehensive training programmes on occupational safety and health. Efforts should be made for the development of appropriate training modules solely on the use of mineral and synthetic fibres which could be incorporated into these comprehensive programmes for different target groups.

53. The experts recognised the problems of employers of small-sized enterprises in taking preventive measures. Many of them might not be aware of the hazards associated with the use of these fibres and find it difficult to take appropriate measures. Support for these enterprises should be provided by the suppliers and the competent authorities especially concerning training in health hazard evaluation and practical control measures.

54. The experts pointed out the large number of persons needed to be trained. In this regard, international co-operation with the ILO support should focus on the development of practical training and information materials and the training of qualified trainers at national and regional levels. Training packages using cost-effective training methods should be developed so that they could be incorporated into various training activities, especially those dealing with chemical risks or dust exposures and occupational health services.

55. The lack of technical expertise was recognised as a factor impeding the organisation of training activities in many countries. The experts considered that the ILO's assistance was needed in training both specialists dealing with the issue at the national level and non-specialist trainers who could multiply the training effects.

Review of the revised working paper

56. The meeting reviewed the revised working paper on safety in the use of mineral and synthetic fibres and recommended its publication by the ILO.

Conclusions and recommendations

57. The meeting made the following conclusions and recommendations:

(1) The experts appreciated the assessment made by the International Programme on Chemical Safety (IPCS) concerning man-made mineral fibres, as requested by the resolution adopted by the 72nd Session of the International Labour Conference, which was a useful basis for the meeting. In view of a continuing need for further evaluation concerning other fibres, the experts supported the point of the resolution requesting the health risk assessment of synthetic organic fibres by the IPCS. This assessment needs to be expedited.

(2) The experts agreed to retain the definition of a respirable fibre in conformity with that used in the ILO code of practice, Safety in the use of asbestos, and other documents. The experts expressed concern, however, that this definition of respirable fibres did not adequately describe those fibres which were currently thought to pose a significant hazard. The meeting believed that a redefinition was needed.

(3) The experts noted the need for establishing through an international body such as the IPCS a standardised set of procedures for the laboratory evaluation of toxicological effects associated with the use of mineral and synthetic fibres.

(4) The experts underlined the importance of providing all people concerned with practical advice on preventive and control measures in production and use of mineral and synthetic fibres to minimise their potentially harmful effects on health. To this end, the working paper on safety in the use of mineral and synthetic fibres, revised by this meeting, should be urgently published by the ILO.

(5) The ILO should collect and disseminate information on health risks and control measures related to mineral and synthetic fibres particularly through the International Occupational Safety and Health Information Centre (CIS) and its network.

(6) The experts pointed out the need for early dissemination of new information on health risks or new and effective control measures associated with the use of the large variety of mineral and synthetic fibres. Such information, including unpubl hed data, should be exchanged making more use of the ILO International Occupational Safety and Health Hazard Alert System.

8612d

(7) The experts recommended that the ILO should prepare and adopt as early as possible a code of practice on safety in the use of insulation wools (glasswool, rockwool and slagwool). Such a code should cover the potential hazards of these fibres, the protection of workers against those hazards, and their safe use and handling.

(8) The experts noted that the adoption of a Convention and a Recommendation concerning safety in the use of mineral and synthetic fibres was premature in view of the lack of enough knowledge on many of these fibres.

(9) The experts emphasised the importance of developing technical co-operation activities particularly in developing countries through the ILO to strengthen capabilities especially for evaluating health risks of mineral and synthetic fibres, taking preventive and control measures, monitoring the working environment and training people concerned.

(10) The experts emphasised the key role of education and training in promoting safety in the use of mineral and synthetic fibres and recommended the development of appropriate training packages with modules applicable to various target groups.

(11) The experts recommended to the Governing Body of the ILO to take the foregoing into account when formulating the Programme and Budget proposals for the 1992-93 biennium.

LIST OF PARTICIPANTS

<u>Experts</u>

Mr. O.A. Akinniranye   Director,
Mains Ventures Ltd.,
PO Box 730,
<u>IKORODU</u>
Lagos State

(Nigeria)

Dr. H. Behrens   Wissenschaftlicher Mitarbeiter,
Bundesanstalt für Arbeitsschutz,
Postfach 170202
4600 <u>DORTMUND</u>

(Federal Republic of Germany)

Mr. S. Dixon   Occupational Health Consultant,
E.I. Du Pont de Nemours & Co.,
N11502,
1007 Market Street,
<u>WILMINGTON</u>
Delaware 19898

(United States)

Professor P. Elmes   Consultant in Occupational Lung
Diseases,
Dawros House,
St. Andrews Road,
<u>DINAS POWYS</u>
South Glamorgan CF6 4HB

(United Kingdom)

Dr. K. Esser   European Mineral Fibres Association,
Grünzweig & Hartmann Glasfaser AG,
Bürgermeister-Grünzweig-Strasse 1,
6700 <u>LUDWIGSHAFEN</u>

(Federal Republic of Germany)

Mr. H. Goto	Director, Working Environment Improvement Office, Industrial Safety and Health Department, Labour Standards Bureau, Ministry of Labour, 1-2-2 Kasumigaseki, Chiyoda-ku TOKYO 100 (Japan)
Mr. K.C. Gupta	Director-General, Factory Advice Service & Labour Institutes, Central Labour Institute, N.S. Mankiker Marg, Sion, BOMBAY 400 022 (India)
Dr. A. Khalef	Cité Inforba, Bt A2 No. 10, Rouiba, 35300 BOUMERDES (Algeria)
Mr. K.D. Klaua	Freier Deutscher Gewerkschaftsbund, 70 Fritz-Heckert Strasse, 1026 BERLIN (German Democratic Republic)
Dr. H.H. Lim	Director, Mediviron Consultants, c/o Malaysian Employers' Federation, PO Box 11026, 50732 KUALA LUMPUR (Malaysia)

8612d

Ms. B. Meek	Senior Evaluator, Environmental Health Directorate, Environmental Health Centre, Room 204, Tunney's Pasture, OTTAWA Ontario K1A OL2 (Canada)
Dr. N.N. Molodkina (Ms.)	Research Institute for Labour Hygiene & Occupational Diseases, Prospekt Budennogo 31, 105 275 MOSCOW (USSR)
Mr. S.W. Samuels	American Federation of Labour and Congress of Industrial Organisations, 815 Sixteenth Street, WASHINGTON DC 20006 (United States)
Mr. Amin Suggun	Malaysian Trade Union Congress, PO Box 38, PETALING JAYA (Malaysia)
Dr. P. Westerholm	Confederation of Swedish Trade Unions (LO), Barnhusgatan 18, 10553 STOCKHOLM (Sweden)

Advisers to the experts

Dr. J. Dunnigan
Adviser to Ms. Meek

Director,
Health and Environment,
The Asbestos Institute,
Pavillon Marie-Victorin,
Suite 336,
Sherbrooke University,
SHERBROOKE
Quebec JIK 2R1

   (Canada)

Mr. A. Ignatow
Adviser to Ms. Meek

Acting Director,
Mineral Policy Sector,
Department of Energy, Mines and
   Resources,
580 Booth Street, 6th Floor,
OTTAWA
Ontario K1A OE4

   (Canada)

Mr. M. Kurilin
Adviser to Ms. Molodkina

Senior Economist,
State Committee for Labour,
Department of International
   Relations,
MOSCOW

   (USSR)

Dr. J.W. Rothuizen
Adviser to Mr. Dixon

Director, Rothuizen Consulting,
"En Thiéré"
1261 GENOLIER, Vd.

   (Switzerland)

Mr. H. Tiesler
Adviser to Dr. Esser

Grünzweig & Hartmann A.G.,
Bürgermeister-Grünzweig-Strasse 1,
6700 LUDWIGSHAFEN

   (Federal Republic of Germany)

Representatives of inter-
governmental organisations

World Health Organization

Professor F. Valic,
Vice Rector,
Andrija Stampar School of
   Occupational Health,
Zagreb University,
Rockfellerova 4,
41000 ZAGREB

(Yugoslavia)

Representatives of non-
governmental international
organisations

International Commission
   on Occupational Health

Dr. Marianne Saux
Saint Gobain "Les Miroirs",
18 avenue d'Alsace,
92096 PARIS

(France)

International Confedera-
tion of Free Trade
Unions

Mr. E. Laurijssen,
Director,
ICFTU,
rue Montagne aux herbes
   potagères 37-41,
1000 BRUXELLES

(Belgium)

International Organisa-
tion of Employers

Miss B. Perkins,
Assistant to the Secretary-General,
International Organisation of
   Employers,
PO Box 68,
1216 GENEVE

(Switzerland)

Mr. A. Buoli,
Engineer,
Balzaretti Modigliani,
SpA,
Viale B. Romagnoli 6,
20146 MILANO

(Italy)

Mr. M. Falk,
Deputy Head,
Working Environment Department,
Danish Employers' Confederation,
PO Box 386,
1503 COPENHAGEN

(Denmark)

Mr. J. Meijers,
Medical Adviser,
Rockwool Lapinus BV,
PO Box 1160,
6040 KD ROERMOND

(Netherlands)

International Social
    Security Association

Dr. A. Oberhansberg,
Berufsgenossenschaft der chemischen
    Industrie,
Gaisbergstrasse 11,
Postfach 101 480,
6900 HEIDELBERG

(Federal Republic of Germany)

World Confederation of
    Labour

Mr. L. Dusoleil,
Ocidergemselaan 26-32,
1040 BRUXELLES

(Belgium)

Mrs. B. Fauchère,
World Confederation of Labour,
1 rue de Varembé,
Case postale 122,
1211 GENEVE 20

(Switzerland)

World Federation of
Trade Unions

Mr. A. Potapov,
Permanent Representative,
World Federation of Trade Unions,
10 rue Fendt,
1201 GENEVE

(Switzerland)

Observers

The Asbestos International
Association

Mr. D. Bouige,
Association française de l'Amiante,
10 rue de la Pépinière,
75008 PARIS

(France)

European Insulation Manu-
facturers' Association

Dr. H. Grimm,
EURIMA,
avenue Louise 137,
bte 8,
1050 BRUXELLES

(Belgium)

Mr. I. Ohberg,
EURIMA;
avenue Louise 137,
bte 8,
1050 BRUXELLES

(Belgium)

International Federation of Building and Wood-workers	Mr. E. Laub, Research Officer, IFBWW, 27-29 rue de la Coulouvrenière, 1204 GENEVE (Switzerland)
International Federation of Chemical, Energy and General Workers' Union	Mr. E. Lechelt, IG Chemie-Papier-Keramik, Königsworther Platz 6, 3000 HANOVER (Federal Republic of Germany)
International Textile, Garment and Leather Workers' Federation	Mr. E. Brombart, ITGLWF, 8 rue Joseph Stevens 1000 BRUXELLES (Belgium)
Joint European Medical Research Board	Professor C.E. Rossiter, London School of Hygiene and Tropical Medicine, Keppel Street, LONDON WCIE 7HT (United Kingdom) Dr. O. Kamstrup, Occupational Physician, Rockwool A/S, 2640 HEDEHUSENE (Denmark)
Thermal Insulation Manufacturers' Association	Dr. F.J. Rauscher Jr., Executive Director, Thermal Insulation Manufacturers' Association, 29 Bank Street, STAMFORD Ct. 06093 (United States)

Dr. J. Konzen,
Owens-Corning Fiberglas,
Fiberglas Tower,
TOLEDO
Ohio 43659

    (United States)

Dr. R. Anderson,
Manville Corporation,
PO Box 5108,
DENVER
Colorado 80202

    (United States)

Mr. D. Samson,
Manville Corporation,
PO Box 5108,
DENVER
Colorado 80202

    (United States)

Mr. K. Gould,
Owens Corning Fiberglas.
Fiberglas Tower,
TOLEDO
Ohio 43659

    (United States)

Dr. R. Mast,
Carbonundum Company,
PO Box 156,
345 3rd Street,
NIAGARA FALLS
New York 14302

    (United States)

Trade Unions International of Workers of the Building, Wood and Building Materials Industries

Mr. J. d'Angelo,
Fédération nationale des Travailleurs
  de la Construction,
Case 413,
263 rue de Paris,
99514 MONTREUIL Cédex

(France)